Innovating
with Impact

Innovating with Impact

Ted Ladd and Alessandro Lanteri

INNOVATING WITH IMPACT

Published with permission from *The Economist* by Pegasus Books.

The Economist is an imprint of
Pegasus Books, Ltd.
148 West 37th Street, 13th Floor
New York, NY 10018

ISBN: 978-1-63936-361-2

10 9 8 7 6 5 4 3 2

Printed in the United States of America
Distributed by Simon & Schuster
www.pegasusbooks.com

PEGASUS BOOKS
NEW YORK LONDON

To the unsung innovators whose products make our lives better every day: comfortable office chairs, electric scooters and microwaveable dishware to name a few.

To our students, including our executive education clients, who strive individually so that we can thrive collectively.

To our spouses, who teach us how to become the people that you think we can be, which is higher than what we would or could envision for ourselves. And who let us sit endlessly in the comfortable chairs to write, ride the electric scooters to work at dawn, and ignore how much microwaveable food we eat when you're not looking.

Contents

Introduction:
Innovation everywhere

In 1815, the volcano Mount Tambora in Indonesia erupted, throwing enough ash into the atmosphere to block sunlight from reaching the earth. The event pushed much of the planet into a premature winter, precipitating a significant crop failure across Northern Europe in 1816. With limited fodder, farmers opted to feed cows, which could supply food, instead of horses, which were used primarily for transportation. People were forced to walk instead of ride, requiring more time and energy to travel.

Two years later, Karl von Drais mounted a flat board between two wooden wheels a few feet apart. His device allowed a person to sit astride the board and plant their feet on the ground to run uphill or lift their feet to coast downhill. In front of a large crowd, he demonstrated that his *laufmaschine* (running machine) could go 7km (4.3 miles) in an hour. Ironically, this was considered too fast, causing this first incarnation of the bicycle to be outlawed in several cities for creating a hazard to pedestrians.

Karl von Drais was not an engineer or a mechanic, but he was an avid inventor. He demonstrated that *anyone can innovate with impact*. We tend to think that innovation is the preserve of a special few introverted geniuses, driven by "Eureka!" moments and instantly resulting in brilliant new products. In our long experience and research, innovation is not confined to a subset of preternaturally gifted people. By describing some simple tools, traits and methods, this book will help everyone in business – across every function and level – to improve how they, their teams and their organisations can make a difference through innovation.

The bicycle was a significant innovation, as was the car, the jet engine, the mobile phone and the laptop. Yet an innovation need not be a life-changing product or service. It simply represents something new or a new way of making or using something. For us, the definition of innovation is much more straightforward: *innovation creates customer value by solving customer problems.*

Another everyday item – the mirror in a lift – illustrates how this is so. Originally invented by Archimedes, the man-powered lift used ropes and winches in ancient Rome to hoist gladiators and animals into the Colosseum. Its modern incarnation was introduced in 1885 to support an innovation – steel-framed high-rise buildings – that offered an efficient way to develop residential units in crowded city centres. But one problem undermined the appeal of high-rise buildings: the residents hated the lifts. They found them too slow. At peak hours, waiting for and then using the lift became a frustrating experience. The time spent idly standing in the lobby and then inside the lift seemed interminable.

A faster lift was not the solution. In 1885, riding a cage lift that moved fast was not for the faint-hearted. Installing more lifts was too costly and would address only the waiting time, not the riding time. Ingenious developers finally recognised that residents would accept waiting for and riding in lifts if they had something interesting to look at. And the image that people found most fascinating was ... themselves. So they installed mirrors inside the lifts and in the lobby where people waited. To this day, most lifts have mirrors (or more recently, television screens) inside and out to keep passengers distracted. The mirror wasn't new but using it to make lifts more palatable was. The use of mirrors in a lift solved a customer problem.

There are many other materials that could have been applied to the inside of the lift that would have been novel. I have never seen sandpaper or blinding lights inside a lift. Although new, those would not have addressed the customer need. They would have been inventive but not innovative.

The example of the lift also demonstrates that *everything can be used more innovatively.*

Innovation can be applied to every aspect of a product or service. Consider cars. BMW manufactures and sells cars; Avis rents cars; Uber helps people rent out their own time to drive their car for passengers; and Waymo makes self-driving cars. All four companies offer personal transportation centred around cars. Yet they deliver the value of transportation to the customer in radically different ways, showing us that *every part of a service can be innovated.*

Innovation can be as simple as putting two wheels and an extendable handle on a suitcase or as complex as transforming a suitcase into a smart device with built-in wireless technology, fingerprint locking and self-driving wheels. However, not all innovations rely on more features or higher quality. Sometimes innovations deliver inferior quality, but in a way that is significantly faster, more convenient or less inexpensive than a product with more features. These innovations can be more valuable to customers than existing products or services. The *laufmaschine* was not as good as a horse, because the riders had to push it with their own legs. Yet it was convenient and inexpensive at a time when horses had become scarce and unaffordable.

Innovation pyramid

Profitable innovation rarely arrives in the innovator's mind by epiphany. The trope of some tortured, Eureka-yelling entrepreneur sitting bolt upright in bed in the middle of the night and then jotting down the precise sketch of a billion-pound idea is entertaining but mythical. Innovation is not an extraordinary event, but the outcome of a deliberate process.

We think of innovation as a pyramid, as seen in Figure 1.

It must rest on solid foundations of culture and individual mindset. Company – and even national – characteristics of openness, agility and ambidexterity provide a cultural context that promotes innovation. Personal traits like curiosity, objectivity, flexibility, adaptability and grit all enhance innovativeness. People who embrace the right attitudes are not guaranteed to be successful in innovation, but people who show none of these characteristics are probably doomed to an uninnovative future. These foundations are empirically more likely to lead to the adoption of a process for innovation, which is then more likely to generate an innovative idea. We discuss this foundation in Part 1 of this book.

At the next level of the innovation pyramid are processes, tools and methods that intentionally promote new opportunities. These encourage new ideas, identify sources of authentic value, refine existing products and services, or develop new ones that can deliver value. Such processes and techniques transform ideation from a freak event into a serious

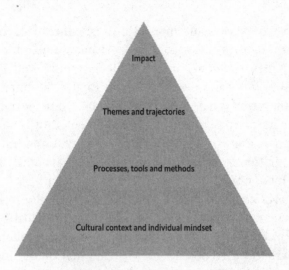

Figure 1. The innovation pyramid

game of probabilities. Resources of people and money are then made available to move ideas to prototypes and then to actual products or services. Part 2 of this book examines what is needed at this level of the pyramid.

Many contemporary efforts to innovate converge towards some common themes and trajectories that we have been cataloguing. In recent years, companies have found huge success by creating multi-sided platforms, by experimenting with novel pricing that descends all the way to "free", by collecting and analysing large data sets with artificial intelligence, and by recognised innovations that benefit not just company profits but also communities and societies. These examples can provide inspirational cases for other innovators to amend and adapt to new markets. We cover this in Part 3.

At the summit of the pyramid sits *impact*, the ultimate

purpose of successful innovation. The thread of impact runs through each part of this book, but we give it special attention in the concluding section. Although we want to demystify innovation, we don't want to give the impression that innovation is trite or inconsequential. Quite the opposite. We are deeply passionate about the potential of innovation to improve the world and we hope many will find this book an inspiration to innovate with a purpose that contributes to better humankind.

Innovating with Impact describes each of the layers of this pyramid with examples across a range of industries and geographies. Each chapter is self-contained: readers can jump around the book for the insights that matter most to accelerating innovations within their own organisations.

Humans have been innovating for 200,000 years. It is baked into our genes, quite fortunately. We innovate for the love of innovating. No one working on an innovation knows where it will end up, what contribution to humanity it might make, or what further evolution it might go through. We are sure Karl von Drais never imagined how his simple running board with two wheels would one day morph through countless innovations into the amazingly sophisticated carbon fibre 21-gear bike, the 35-mile per hour electric bike, or the internationally popular Harley Davidson motorcycle. But it isn't necessary to be clairvoyant to innovate.

We want this book to show how everyone can use the traits and techniques we discuss to support innovation both for business success and to contribute to making life on this planet easier, more productive and more enjoyable.

PART 1

The context and mindset for innovation

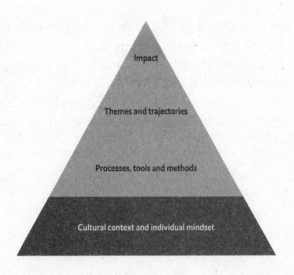

In times of rapid change, people and organisations must innovate ever more rapidly just to keep up. In such times, innovation is no longer a nice to have. It becomes an essential capability to remain effective and a key ingredient for continued success. This is not a challenge. It is an opportunity.

The good news is that anyone can innovate. Yet not everyone does. Innovation can happen anywhere, but it doesn't happen everywhere.

While daring innovators and innovative organisations surely have something unique about them, they are not blessed with some mystical magic ingredient. The mindsets and the conditions that make them successful at innovating are well known, they can be recognised and measured and – most importantly – they can be nurtured and improved by anyone.

The first part of this book covers the foundations of innovation. The individual traits that make individual innovators stand out are covered in Chapter 1. Chapter 2 highlights aspects of organisations that make the strategic decisions and create the cultural conditions that empower their employees to innovate.

With this, we want to invite you to explore how to become a better innovator and help others become better innovators at work and beyond.

1

Innovative people

The start-up Confinity began in Silicon Valley as a simple idea. Just as people can hand a physical dollar bill from one person to another, they should be able to "beam" a dollar from one smartphone to another. In 1998, three people in Silicon Valley invented a piece of software that could send money from one PalmPilot to another.

The devices from Palm were precursors to the contemporary smartphone. In the 1990s, however, they did not have the capability for an internet connection. To beam money from one device to the another, the people needed to be about two feet apart. This was an interesting and elegant technical solution, but it lacked a fundamental element in its business model: a person holding a Palm device would probably have a wallet full of dollars. Exchanging physical dollars was easier, faster and safer than using this software.

The innovators continued to search for potential sources of growth. They even approached one of the authors of this book (Ted), who at that time was an employee at Palm tasked with helping the software developers to create new innovations for the PalmPilot. Ted concluded that the idea would never find traction.

With hindsight, Ted and the entire world now know that

his prediction was short-sighted and less than visionary. A year later, the founders of Confinity – Max Levchin, Peter Thiel and Luke Nosek – launched a working electronic payments system and shortly thereafter sold the company to X.com, founded by Elon Musk. Thiel soon replaced Musk as CEO, renamed the company PayPal in 2000 and in 2002 took the company public, garnering $61m through its initial public offering. Only months later, Thiel sold PayPal to eBay for $1.5bn. PayPal is now one of the largest digital payment platforms in the world.

Clearly, innovation does not happen by itself. Someone, an imperfect human being, must be searching for novel ways to create customer value. What traits within the founders of Confinity propelled them to persist and to evolve their idea? What makes some innovators more likely to find success than others?

The most successful innovators have an "innovator's mindset". It may be that some people are born with this mindset, but the elements of it are complex enough to lead us to believe that it is a set of cognitive and emotional characteristics that can be developed over time by anyone. Research into entrepreneurship reveals that this mindset has three key elements: orientation, self-efficacy and objectivity. Here's a look at each of them.

Entrepreneurial orientation

Entrepreneurial orientation (EO) emerged from academic research in the early 1990s as a powerful predictor of venture success. People who showed this complex trait were more likely to start and grow new companies. EO is not a single characteristic. One of the seminal articles in this field was written in 1996 by G.T. Lumpkin at Northeastern State University and Gregory Dess at the University of Texas.[1] Over the past 30 years, scholars have determined that EO encompasses a set of five traits that successful innovators have in greater amounts than people who rarely innovate. Innovators always have at least some degree of these traits, though the amount of each trait and the combination can vary. Read the descriptions here and then take the self-test that follows to assess your own EO.

- *Innovativeness* refers to the ability to generate new ideas, be they products, processes or technologies. This quality has long been a durable trait in entrepreneurial research, harking back to economist Joseph Schumpeter who, in 1942, introduced the concept of "creative destruction", by which he noted how entrepreneurial innovation periodically overtakes the status quo in business, replacing current products and processes with new technologies. Schumpeter believed that a definite entrepreneurial spirit (*unternehmergeist*) was necessary to innovate and that people working in companies that invest in innovation ultimately drive the economy forward.

- *Autonomy* relates to an innovator's sense of independence to take a strategic initiative, disengaged from any surrounding bureaucracy, to explore a new venture. For those who work in hierarchical command-and-control companies, the innovator might be considered a "maverick" who refuses to adhere to the rules and conventions of the company's policies and processes. Once involved in an innovation start-up venture, the person may continue to exhibit this same strong autonomy and may even be seen as autocratic, imposing their vision on others in the new venture.

- *Risk-taking* captures the trait that entrepreneurs need to have to take action in the face of uncertainty. Risk-taking may involve making financial and other resource commitments with no guarantee of payback or profit. This characteristic does not mean that innovators do not assess risks or consider them in their decision-making; they do. Innovators determine that such risks are worth taking because they can envision success.

- *Proactivity* reflects the entrepreneur's desire and drive to seize any first-mover advantage possible to shape a new market. This quality affects the innovator's sense of speed in wanting to get things done as quickly as possible and their sense of time to be in the marketplace before anyone else.

- *Aggressiveness* refers to an innovator's sense of intensity and posturing during head-to-head competition with any other product, service or technology that is deemed a rival. It is simply the quality of being a competitive personality, unwilling to let anyone else win. Aggressiveness differs from proactivity in that proactivity looks at unoccupied market space, whereas aggressiveness assumes existing competition.

Testing your entrepreneurial orientation

You can assess your EO using the following self-test. For each question in Part 1, indicate your agreement on a scale of 1 to 5, where 1 reflects strong disagreement and 5 reflects strong agreement.

Part 1	Disagree ⟶ Agree				
I like high-risk projects with the potential of very high returns (Risk)	1	2	3	4	5
I enjoy exploring new ideas (Risk)	1	2	3	4	5
I actively improve and innovate in my professional career (Innovativeness)	1	2	3	4	5
I am creative (Innovativeness)	1	2	3	4	5
I seek new ways to do things (Innovativeness)	1	2	3	4	5
I try to speak and act first when working with others (Proactivity)	1	2	3	4	5
I excel at identifying new opportunities (Proactivity)	1	2	3	4	5
I initiate actions to which other people respond (Proactivity)	1	2	3	4	5
I am proactive (Proactivity)	1	2	3	4	5
I am intensely competitive (Aggressiveness)	1	2	3	4	5
I am bold and aggressive (Aggressiveness)	1	2	3	4	5
I aim to outmanoeuvre and "undo the competition" in my business ventures (Aggressiveness)	1	2	3	4	5
I embrace bold, wide-ranging acts to achieve my objectives (Aggressiveness)	1	2	3	4	5
I prefer to act and think without interference (Autonomy)	1	2	3	4	5
I work independently (Autonomy)	1	2	3	4	5
I do not like authority (Autonomy)	1	2	3	4	5
Total of Part 1					

For Part 2, the scale is reversed. Strong agreement merits a 1 and strong disagreement merits a 5.

Part 2	Agree ———————→ Disagree				
I prefer low-risk projects (RiskR)	1	2	3	4	5
I am cautious (RiskR)	1	2	3	4	5
I respond to actions from competitors (ProactivityR)	1	2	3	4	5
I look to others for new ideas (ProactivityR)	1	2	3	4	5
I emphasise solutions that have already been tried and have been proven successful (InnovativenessR)	1	2	3	4	5
Total of Part 2					

Scoring your EO

When you have scored these statements, add the totals from Part 1 and Part 2. Then divide by 21 to calculate an average score, which should be between 1 and 5. This is your EO score.

Note that the five dimensions of entrepreneurial orientation are not cumulative. Some of them overlap and reflect the same underlying trait. For example, people who like to take risks also typically like personal autonomy. Thus, an individual's entrepreneurial orientation can be evaluated using the five dimensions, but is often summarised and interpreted as a single trait based on the average of your responses to all the questions.

In an academic paper in 2018, Ted, along with fellow Hult professors Joanne Lawrence and Patricia Hind, analysed 1,859 students and found that the average across all five characteristics of entrepreneurial orientation was 3.80 on the scale of 1 to 5.[2] Those with a higher score were more likely to start new businesses and more likely to succeed with those new ventures.

It is important to note that entrepreneurial orientation is not a conclusive measure by which to predict your potential success as an innovator. EO scores vary greatly across age, gender, cultures and region of origin. In some national cultures and corporate environments, being a risk-taker or an autonomous thinker is severely frowned upon and even discouraged. Being proactive or competitive is perceived as anti-social behaviour. Thus, depending on where you are from, your gender or age, getting a score of 2.0 does not doom you to failure as an innovator. Indeed, this score might be high in some populations that culturally do not foster or appreciate entrepreneurial behaviour. Even more importantly, your score for entrepreneurial orientation can increase as you gain wisdom, skills and experience.

Now that you understand the concept of EO and have your own EO score, how does this help you innovate? If you have a relatively high EO score, your existing innate characteristics already give you a foundation for generating impactful innovations. You are ready to move to the next step. If you have a relatively low EO score, you have two options. The first is to select areas of innovation that lie within your own scope. For example, if you are aggressive but not proactive, this suggests that you are reactive. Reactive innovators search for flaws in existing products such that a customer's problems are not entirely addressed. Moreover, a reactive innovator might only find motivation for innovation when solving a problem that they personally encounter. The innovator is finding a solution in order to be the first beneficiary.

The second option if you have a low EO score is to find or build the right context for you to innovate. You might assemble a team of people who, together, might encompass many of the crucial traits of EO. An individual who is inherently innovative but not autonomous should find a business partner who seeks and thrives with independence from an overarching organisation. Or you might move to an organisation that recognises and rewards risk-taking.

Just by knowing that the concept of entrepreneurial orientation exists will help you see the set of traits in yourself and in others. This observation might even by itself provoke a change in your own beliefs and behaviours. In other words, understanding EO might create EO.

Self-efficacy

The second element of the innovator's mindset is self-efficacy, which is broadly similar to self-confidence but with an important distinction. Whereas self-confidence is often used to reflect a person's overall aura, self-efficacy is much more specific. It describes a person's confidence in their ability to achieve a specific goal by taking a specific action in a specific circumstance.

For example, after years of teaching innovation to business school students, we have a high degree of self-efficacy in our ability to empower students with skills in innovation that they will use effectively after graduation to bring new, impactful ideas into the marketplace. But that doesn't mean that we are confident about all aspects of business. The intricacies of double-entry accounting still baffle us. Nor are we confident about our ability to generate innovations in medicine or architecture were we to work with students in those disciplines. Our self-efficacy is narrowing, contained within a specific domain with a specific set of outcomes.

Self-efficacy is not the same as competence. Self-efficacy is a subjective perception. Competence is an objective assessment. Self-efficacy without competence is arrogance. Using our example again, it is possible for professors to have a high personal degree of self-efficacy for student outcomes that does not match their skill in teaching.

However, self-efficacy often generates competence. A person with confidence in an activity is more likely to practise that behaviour continually, typically leading to an improvement in the result. Professors with self-efficacy in teaching innovation will continue to teach, collect evidence on their impact, and make improvements in their content and technique. Through practice, they will almost certainly improve their impact.

Over the last 15 years, management scholars involved in studying innovation have examined the role of self-efficacy in greater detail. They find that specific actions can bolster self-efficacy and lead to successful entrepreneurial activity. Jeffrey McGee, a professor at the University of Texas, found a specific type of self-efficacy that he labelled "entrepreneurial self-efficacy for searching", which refers to the confidence that a person has in their own ability to find a new idea that will blossom into an innovative, impactful product or company.

Why does this matter? Because an innovator's mindset makes impactful innovation more likely. Building one's own self-efficacy for searching contributes to that mindset. In Ted's 2018 paper (mentioned above), there were significant variations in the degree of self-efficacy according to age, gender and national origin. Nonetheless, the links between a student's sense of self-efficacy and their ability to search for a new business idea were strong.

Self-efficacy self-test

Here are questions to ask yourself to determine your score for self-efficacy as it relates to the two steps of searching and marshalling.

	How much confidence do you have in yourself to:	Not much ⟶ A lot				
Searching	come up with a new idea or service?	1	2	3	4	5
	identify the need for a new product or service?	1	2	3	4	5
	design a product or service that will satisfy customer needs and wants?	1	2	3	4	5
Marshalling	get others to identify with and believe in your vision and plans for the future?	1	2	3	4	5
	network, i.e. make contact and exchange information with others?	1	2	3	4	5
	clearly and concisely explain your business idea in everyday terms (verbally or in writing)?	1	2	3	4	5
	Total your scores					
	Divide by 6 to find your average score					

The average score among the sample of almost 1,700 students was 4.2 out of 5. Like many cognitive traits, self-efficacy is mutable and mercurial. It can be affected by slow-moving influences like one's culture, but also by transient influences such as mood and recent experience in innovation. It is even more influenced by experience than the traits of entrepreneurial orientation discussed earlier. Serial entrepreneurs might see only small movements around their appetite for risk, for example. Yet a few initial successful innovations will produce a dramatic increase in entrepreneurial self-efficacy. A few initial failures will have the opposite impact.

Now that you understand the importance of self-efficacy, what can you do about it? Albert Bandura at Stanford University, the originator of the concept of self-efficacy, has offered numerous suggestions for developing and improving it.[3] First, a person, along with their mentors and peers, can set moderately challenging but attainable goals to experience the challenge – and triumph – of small achievements in innovation. Second, innovators can find and recruit role models and mentors in their specific target domain. Someone hoping to innovate within the realm of hospitality, for example, can find managers and leaders in the industry to emulate. Finally, self-efficacy relies on self-reflection. Someone hoping to improve their confidence about their own impact should document and then refer to the lessons from each success, failure and external observation. Self-efficacy can be built upon evidence of success, which requires that an innovator solicit and internalise such evidence.

Both of us teach innovation to graduate students. Part of the success of our classes is built upon our ability to convince students that, as a result of the class, they have the skills to innovate with impact. In other words, we are not just teaching them the methods. We are also giving them the confidence to employ these methods, which makes them more likely to practise these methods in the real world. By trying the methods, these students can improve them.

We build student self-efficacy for innovating using Bandura's model. We set assignments for the class that push each student to try something slightly out of their comfort zone. When they take even a small step towards innovation, we applaud them loudly and publicly. This is not false or inauthentic praise. They have done something courageous.

We engineer opportunities to congratulate them. Second, we mentor these students through personal relationships that give them individualised attention and support. Third, because both of us have had success as innovators, we offer ourselves as role models to these students. We also bring many guest speakers into our classes. Across all these interactions, most of our students find a person that they can admire and emulate. Finally, we force students to reflect on their actions towards learning to innovate – actions that were successful and those that were not. We do not do this with any judgement about their value as a human being. We do not belittle or harangue.

We assume that a person without self-efficacy for innovation is not doomed to poor innovations. Instead, we assume that such people need a more supportive context to allow them to internalise the methods of innovation into their own confidence that these methods will work.

Objectivity

Entrepreneurial orientation and self-efficacy reflect what people think about themselves. These are purely subjective assessments. Two people with very different beliefs about themselves may still behave in the same way despite their subjective assessments. Subjectivity is unavoidable for assessing traits but it is lethal when assessing capacity for successful innovation. That is why an innovator's mindset needs a third element: objectivity.

Objectivity is the voice of other people's wisdom when going through the steps of innovation. Not every idea is brilliant, valid, usable or even worthy of further pursuit. Being able to recognise when an idea will lead to a dead end or has no chance of meeting consumer needs can save innovators a lot of time and resources.

Objectivity is the antidote to natural human weaknesses. When contemplating a new idea, many people fall into one or both of twin traps: confirmation bias and selection bias. *Confirmation bias* describes a behaviour where the actor ignores any new information that runs counter to existing beliefs. We literally hear and recognise only information that confirms what we already believe to be true. Later in this book, we will talk about deliberate strategies to reduce the tendency towards confirmation for new ideas. The impact of such strategies depends on one's own comfort in being wrong, being able to listen to and act on information. An innovator's objectivity is necessary to realise that sandpaper on the walls of a lift might be new but not useful; inventive but not innovative.

There are two common avenues to reduce confirmation bias. The first is actively to seek information that would *invalidate* an idea. Instead of attempting to find supporting logic and facts, an objective innovator starts the process with a search for logic and facts that might poke holes in the value of an idea. This practice relates to self-efficacy in searching for an entrepreneurial idea. Someone who is confident that they can eventually find and develop a fruitful innovation has the emotional strength and persistence to put the idea immediately through a pressure cooker of potentially unflattering experiments.

Confirmation bias commonly leads to a second bias, *selection bias*, where someone seeking feedback on an idea chooses to solicit opinions from a group of friends who are predisposed to agree. This audience will incorporate their desire to please the speaker into their opinion about the innovation at issue.

It is not enough to approach strangers for their opinions. An aggressively objective innovation, buoyed by entrepreneurial orientation and self-efficacy in searching for a new idea, might do well to seek out feedback even from people who have well-known alternative interests.

As an illustration, let's talk about parking spaces. Like the cliff swallows returning to Capistrano every March, every year one of our students will declare that they have the perfect business: a service through a smartphone (that is, an app) that will help match people who are looking for a parking spot for their car with a person who owns an empty parking space. Because such a service does not currently exist in their home city and seems logical and valuable at first glance, they are convinced that it will be innovative.

Unfortunately, this product is unlikely to deliver the value to customers that these students anticipate. First, there is the enormous cost of making drivers and parking lot owners aware of the app such that they download it to their smartphone and consult it. Second is the "chicken-or-egg" problem that is common to multi-sided platforms: if a driver consults the app and does not find an available parking space, the driver is unlikely to consult the app again. If a person who owns an empty parking space opens the app only to find that there are not currently any drivers actively seeking a spot, they are unlikely to take the effort to sign up for the service and update the status of the parking space. And then we get into the issues of security for the car and security for the parking space. And what happens if the driver refuses to leave? Or if the owner suddenly wants the empty space? In summary, this idea is objectively not likely to provide customer value.

An innovator must be willing to take a risk, think innovatively, act autonomously and proactively. An innovator must have confidence in their ability to create new products and services that will eventually solve customer problems. And yet an innovator must also be open to external evidence to test and determine if a particular idea will in fact be impactful.

The innovator's mindset

These three traits – entrepreneurial orientation, self-efficacy, and objectivity – comprise the innovator's mindset. People with these traits are more likely to consider innovating and are more likely to generate innovations that create significant customer value.

It is difficult to know with certainty the degree to which the most well-known innovators of the past decades had all the traits of the innovator's mindset. Despite hundreds of articles and books covering entrepreneurs like Steve Jobs, Marie Curie, Nicola Tesla or Shirley Jackson, we have yet to find the "perfect" innovator's mindset. Jobs launched numerous technology failures when he was CEO of Apple. Musk's first version of PayPal was voted as one of the worst business ideas of its time. Bezos oversaw the development of Amazon's Fire Phone, a total failure.

The past decades have seen thousands of start-ups founded and headed up by highly intelligent and driven entrepreneurs who appeared to have the right components of the innovator's mindset. Innovation is directly, positively and significantly correlated to this attitude. What is more difficult to observe is the number of people who lacked this mindset who did not even attempt to innovate. For this reason, the innovator's mindset remains a predictive but not deterministic characteristic of innovation. If you have it, you are more likely to generate impactful innovation. If you do not have it, you can develop it. If you do not have it and do not develop it, you may still be able to innovate, but the odds are against you.

Empowered with an innovator's mindset, an individual can improve the odds of generating a successful innovation by embedding into a group of people who together can foster innovation. Just as there are traits that predict and accelerate innovation in an individual, there are also traits of an organisation that predict and accelerate the innovation from the team. This topic, organisational innovation, is the focus of the next chapter.

The innovator's brain

Until recently, research into the innovator's mindset has been based on observations about how people behave. A few studies have employed functional magnetic resonance imaging (fMRI) machines to look at the regions of the brain to see how innovators' brains might differ from those of non-innovators, but these machines cannot see minuscule blips of neural activity. There were no theories that could explain how the brain creates new ideas.

The "thousand brains" theory of intelligence from Silicon Valley innovator-turned-scientist Jeff Hawkins is the first proposal to describe how the brain functions at the cellular level.[4] This theory has direct, important and unexpected implications for how people learn to innovate. The first is to expand the number of reference frames that an innovator can call upon. Because the brain starts with available analogies in order to learn a new object, innovators should cram their minds with new historical examples that include an explanation as to why these examples were successful. This helps the brain on a cellular level apply ideas from one context into another. It's an important path to creating something novel and useful.

The second piece of advice from Hawkins revolves around the role of self-efficacy. When new sensory input arrives, all cells compare this new information to their expectations. If all these cells agree that these sensory inputs match the model of something the brain has already understood, they do not need to create a new model. However, if they do not agree, these cells must decide if this is a new detail for an existing model that is already in the brain, or if it is a new object that deserves its own new model. Self-confidence might be construed as the speed and comfort with which the brain makes this decision: more details for an old model or the first details for a new model.

This book intentionally provides hundreds of contemporary and historical examples to give the reader's brain new models of innovation. As the reader is considering new potential innovations, this expanded library will give these new ideas hundreds more reference frames to which the reader can attach these new ideas. Moreover, innovations can emerge from the recombination of existing ideas. By having more models in the brain, the reader can consider new combinations more efficiently and comfortably.

2

Innovative organisations

The expression "It's a Kodak moment" used to be one of the most iconic brand memes in the world. It was universally understood to refer to an unquestionable "perfect" moment in time to take a photo of one's children, spouse, a sunrise, sunset or a stunning natural scene. The film and camera company Eastman Kodak, founded in 1892, had almost single-handedly created the home and professional photography business as well as providing the film stock for nearly the entire Hollywood film industry. In the 1970s, Kodak had about 90% of the photography film production business as well as 85% of camera sales in the United States. The company's Ektachrome slide carousels were as common as toasters in suburban homes, providing evenings of entertainment and memories for families and their friends.

In 1975, one of Kodak's engineers, Steve Sasson, invented the first digital camera. The innovation might have become the next multibillion-dollar product line for Kodak except for one impediment: the senior leadership and board of directors saw no reason to consider this as a useful innovation for the company's photographic film business.[1] Senior Kodak leaders believed that this gave them plenty of time to double down on their commitment to film photography. They simply did not see the train approaching them at the end of the tunnel.

Ironically, Kodak's research team continued to explore digital technology and developed the first megapixel camera in 1986. But Kodak stuck to its convictions that its market leadership in film photography would never end. One new competitor in 1984, the Japanese company Fuji, had introduced colour film at a price 20% cheaper than Kodak, but Kodak believed it was still king of the film business and would not lose much market share to the upstart.

In the next decade, the company did eventually incorporate digital technology, but only in a half-baked way, in 1996 introducing the Advantix Preview camera that allowed users to preview their shot in a digital capture before snapping the photo onto traditional film loaded into the camera. Kodak had invested $500m into the Advantix Preview, believing it would keep the company in the film, chemicals and paper photograph printing business for years to come. However, the Advantix camera failed completely.

In 2004, probably believing better late than never, Kodak withdrew from selling traditional film cameras and began competing with the leading digital camera brands that had already nearly destroyed its business. However, from 2005 to 2010, Kodak's digital cameras failed to gain a major foothold. The company's sales shrunk by 50%, while producing barely any profit. In 2010, Kodak was removed from the S&P 500 list. In 2012, Kodak filed for bankruptcy, with assets of $5.1bn but debts of $6.75bn. A month later, Kodak announced it was leaving the digital camera business completely and would license its name only to other camera manufacturers.

Today, Kodak remains in business, but its primary activity has transferred to the chemical industry. In 2020, President

Trump offered Kodak a $765m loan to manufacture chemicals for use in pharmaceuticals. The goal was to produce more basic chemicals for medicines in the United States rather than continue the heavy reliance on chemicals from China. On news of the final approval for the loan in late 2020, Kodak's stock surged, and it once again had a market capitalisation of $1bn. It was a "Kodak moment" for the company that no longer had a camera or film to record the perfect shot.[2]

The failure of Kodak is a parable of hubris and change-resistant leadership, but also a deep lack of understanding about the value of fostering and mining a corporate culture of innovation. Kodak is not alone in misjudging the need for ongoing innovation when market leader. Think of the once-supreme cellphone firm Research in Motion (later called BlackBerry after its most successful product), whose market dominance in the cellular phone world disappeared due to its failure to innovate at the speed of competitors like Apple and Samsung. Remember the former personal computer superstar Compaq Computer, which led the field in the 1980s and 1990s but fell victim to pricing and service innovations by upstart Dell Computer. HP acquired the failing Compaq in 2002 and tried to revive its reputation, but by 2013 realised that the brand had to be put out to pasture.

There can be no doubt that all these companies had innovative people working for them, but individual innovators are not enough. Just as innovators need to develop an innovator's mindset, companies must also develop a culture that respects innovation and is committed to integrating the best new discoveries that come from its innovators into new products and services.

In recent decades, there has been an evolution of thought on what organisational characteristics are necessary to support innovation. In this chapter, we synthesise five key insights that are seen as among the most important for embedding innovation into corporate culture.

The first of these is to reframe organisational culture into a three-zone mindset – dubbed *three horizons* – that impact the very foundations of the company, from the way management is structured to the tasks and assignments of departments and teams.

The second insight, *ambidexterity*, speaks more directly to the short- and long-term strategic planning within the company.

The third insight emphasises that companies must execute on their strategies with *agility*. This defines what it means to be agile in today's fast-paced, chaotic world and the necessary principles that, if followed, will guide organisations towards that agility.

The fourth insight focuses on how to build the organisation's capabilities to achieve three requirements for innovation: *sensing, seizing and transformation*. These actions together are called "dynamic capabilities" and are at the forefront of academic research into innovation.

Finally, innovative organisations are aware that great ideas can originate anywhere and are willing to engage with the external environment, approaching innovation as an *open* effort and not something to be carried out behind closed doors.

Let's examine each of these insights in detail.

Three horizons

To survive, organisations must sustain consistent profitable growth in their core businesses as well as developing new opportunities for growth on a future timeline. Over time, too many organisations lose sight of how to manage growth such that it proceeds in fits and starts or falters completely. High-performing companies have a mindset based on *three horizons* (see Figure 2).[3]

Horizon 1 is where the organisation must focus its primary efforts. On this horizon are the company's existing profitable core businesses which take centre stage and require the majority of management attention. A company cannot lose sight of providing value to its existing customers through product features, pricing, distribution channels and supply chains. It must pay attention to competitors who might try to best its products or undercut it on price or service benefits. Never losing sight of Horizon 1 ensures that the company can sustain growth through product enhancements in processes, costs and services; losing sight of Horizon 1 is the slippery slope to a slow death.

But Horizon 1 is not the only perspective the company must maintain. It must also work to develop Horizon 2, where emerging opportunities can occur to *extend* its core business. This means paying attention to market trends, new technologies and entrepreneurial competitors. Where possible, the company should use its existing capabilities and existing business models to launch new ideas for its existing customer base, thus lowering risk. Sometimes Horizon 2 requires investing in new entrepreneurial ventures that could generate new products or services that might eventually become the company's Horizon 1 core.

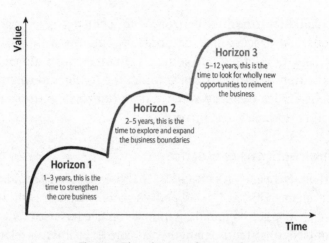

Figure 2. Three horizons framework
Source: M. Baghai, S. Coley and D. White, *The Alchemy of Growth: Practical Insights for Building the Enduring Enterprise* (New York: Perseus Publishing, 1999)

Horizon 3 is where the company must take riskier leaps of faith to explore radical new ideas for growth – be it R&D innovation, partnerships, investments in new ventures, or incubating a group within the company that keeps innovating as if it were a start-up. These efforts are sometimes best put into the hands of the company's mavericks – those who are visionary and have little inclination to follow rules in their pursuit of far-fetched ideas that seem implausible to management. In the context of the company's core business, these efforts seek to produce "disruptive business models" (see Chapter 3). For this reason, Horizon 3 work is often relocated offsite where the radical thinkers are unimpeded by the standard policies, procedures, key performance indicators (KPIs) and incentives that the rest of the company follows while working on Horizons 1 and 2.

Working on the three horizons is not a function of managing sequential processes; it is more like running a three-ring circus with multiple acts going on simultaneously. Constant evaluation of each horizon informs the leadership whether opportunities are ready to move from Horizon 3 to Horizon 2 or from Horizon 2 to Horizon 1.

Three horizons in practice

If there is a paragon example of the three horizons' mindset, one might point at Google and its parent holding company Alphabet. Since its founding in 1998, Google has used its vast profits to consistently strengthen its core H1 businesses related to internet search – including email, browser, advertising and YouTube – while investing in numerous acquisitions that fit the profile of H2 expansions, including its purchase of Motorola Mobility, which allowed Google to enter the mobile phone field with its Android system. Looking far into the future, Google has also invested over the past decade in many acquisitions that one might characterise as long-term H3 investments, including companies involved in robotics, human health and ageing, aerospace, satellites and self-driving technology.

In contrast to Google, consider the fate of the BlackBerry smartphone which once dominated the mobile phone market. Founded in 1999, Research in Motion (which changed its name to BlackBerry in 2013) grew to sales of $20bn by 2011 and a whopping market share of 33%. But by 2016 its market share had decreased to 2.31%. Although the company performed extremely well for more than a decade in its H1 work, and to some extent in its H2 product expansion work, it is often

34

thought that BlackBerry failed to understand the value of exploring and investing in H3 areas. Meanwhile, Apple, Nokia and Samsung were leapfrogging years ahead of BlackBerry in their development of smartphone technologies, applications and design innovation that attracted consumers to see far more value in their smartphones than in the BlackBerry.

What does this concept of multiple horizons matter to innovators? Whereas an innovation might consume an individual's entire attention, a company must create a culture that encourages different individuals and teams to work on multiple different innovations at different stages of development. Not only does this diversify risk away from reliance on a single idea, but it also ensures that a company that launches a successful innovation has yet more innovations under development for subsequent years.

Before you read on, take a moment to consider what this means for you as an innovator. What will your industry be like in ten years' time? Who will your customers be? What will they need? What will they pay for? Now, given these answers, what will you need to be like in ten years to serve those customers? What capabilities and resources will you and your company need?

In an increasingly turbulent and fast-changing world, you cannot safely wait for a decade before you start innovating for the future.

Ambidexterity

No company can focus only on creating and launching new innovations. A company must sell these products or services at scale to generate consistent profits. Michael Tushman of Harvard Business School advises companies to embrace *ambidexterity*.[4]

The literal definition of the term refers to a person who can use both their right and left hands with equal impact when, for example, throwing a ball or playing the piano. Tushman defines corporate ambidexterity as a company's ability to *exploit* its current capabilities and resources while simultaneously *exploring* new territories. Whereas the three horizons concept focuses on exploring new ideas, a culture of ambidexterity reminds us to retain attention on becoming more efficient at selling the company's current product mix.

A commitment to ambidexterity is critical to guarding one's competitive advantage both in the present and future. The paradox is that ambidexterity may require contradictory thinking between the two strategic goals. Exploiting requires a focus on efficiency, cutting costs and a focus on short-term goals to remain competitive; exploring requires a culture of autonomy aimed at long-term goals, expending resources and taking risks. Ambidexterity is thus a balancing act of resources and capabilities to ensure that the organisation maximises its core businesses while devoting equal talent and investment to the intelligent exploration of new opportunities.

Ambidexterity is especially valuable in today's global world where the organisation may be operating in both existing and emerging markets. Existing markets will require more of a strategic focus on exploitation, whereas emerging markets may need the company to be open to exploration through novel ways of doing business, modifications to its products or packaging or different distribution methods.

Four paths to ambidexterity

Boston Consulting Group (BCG) laid out four strategic paths to implementing ambidexterity in a diverse environment, encouraging companies either to employ multiple ambidextrous strategies continuously or switch between them over time.[5]

The first of these is separating business units such that some teams are focused on exploitation and others are working on exploration. A good example of successful separation is PepsiCo, whose multiple traditional and mature brands like Pepsi, Quaker, Tropicana and Gatorade are continuously exploited without lapses. Meanwhile, the company invests in numerous innovative brands to own the reinvention and disruption of its core businesses rather let other firms grab its territory. The problem with separation, however, is that it can create silos. Those who are exploiting neglect to share best practices with those who are exploring. In fast-changing environments, this structural approach to ambidexterity tends to create excessive time lags in bringing innovations to market.

An alternative approach to ambidexterity expects each team to switch from exploration to exploitation and back as the market context changes. Switching can create confusion, resistance and resource conflicts within the organisation, making it difficult to implement in large companies. Materials science company Corning Glass, however, has had some success with this. It quickly transitioned the entire company from exploring glass films for construction and low-tech consumer products to producing its Gorilla Glass product for smartphone screens.

The third approach to ambidexterity, self-organising, is

effective in organisations where small teams or units can self-determine where to put their resources and task emphasis. The Chinese appliance company Haier uses this approach, allowing each of its business units to establish its own operational strategies to maximise its performance. The drawbacks, though, can be duplication of resources and inability to scale up successful innovations.

The fourth approach to ambidexterity taps into external resources, making deals with an ecosystem of partners to provide elements of exploitation or exploration for the company when the environment is too complex for the organisation to do everything on its own. This is, for example, how Apple maintains the innovative edge of its iPhone, leveraging both the scale and reliability of its hardware suppliers and the flexibility and courage of an open ecosystem of apps and software developers.[6]

Agility

The term agility is primarily used to describe the ability of a physical object to adapt to its environment. An agile football player can weave and dodge around obstacles. An agile gymnast can twist around bars and change direction seemingly in mid-air.

The concept of organisational agility refers to an organisation's ability to change direction quickly, from exploitation to exploration and back. The term gained traction in Silicon Valley when it was applied to writing software. The agile method has since spread beyond technology to many areas of product development.

The core principle of the agile approach is to break complex products into smaller tasks that can be accomplished quickly and then shown to the customer. Instead of working for six months on single grand innovations, an agile innovator works for a week on just a small piece of the puzzle and then collects feedback on just that piece. These bursts of work, called sprints, reduce the risk that a team will make an error early in the construction of an innovation, fail to recognise it and continue to expend time and resources on a poor idea.

George Tome, a manager at John Deere which makes heavy machinery for agricultural production, noticed that the time to create and launch a new product relied on both the speed of the team in designing an innovation and the speed of the rest of the organisation in commercialising, scaling, selling and delivering an innovation. Tome concluded that one way to reduce the time between idea and product is to increase the frequency of interactions between innovators, customers and other people in the company. In practice, this means that innovators reveal half-completed projects to stakeholders for feedback. In fact, for more complex products, innovators might solicit opinions at the end of every day, after each tweak to every feature.

At first glance, this approach might seem counterproductive. A potential customer, you might think, could not possibility render useful feedback after seeing only a partial rough draft. Moreover, innovators are not immune from bouts of self-consciousness. They might not want to show half-baked, unpolished work to others. Despite these potential pitfalls, the verdict is in: the agile method works. It generates better products that are more closely matched to customer demands at a faster pace with less investment. In many sectors, the era of "build it and they will come" is over. The new norm relies on fast iterations and frequent feedback.

This agile process has a corresponding recommendation for organisational structure: the direction of an innovation is not dictated by a team leader but instead by customer reaction. This emphasis builds on the importance of objectivity mentioned in Chapter 1.

Introducing "agile"

Just as the agile method recommends a way for teams to innovate, it also recommends a way for companies to introduce the agile method into its own halls. For example, not every team in a company needs to use agile product development principles. A company seeking to consider the approach can introduce it into only one team or function at a time. A top-down edict from upper management for everyone to use an agile process immediately is not an agile approach to innovation.

An example of agile management can be found in the music streaming company Spotify, where management allows teams to choose agile approaches if and how they desire. Many of the more than 70 teams at Spotify apply their own variants of the agile approach, complete with their own forms of progress tracking, rubrics, planning and metrics.

Beyond a process or a structure, the agile method has generated its own cultural norms. First, although different teams can follow different approaches, all the individuals in a team must be on the same page about the goals and approach to innovation. Second, collective intelligence trumps the brilliance of a single player. As a result, recognition and reward systems need to honour entire teams rather than individual efforts. And third, agile cultures respect questions, not orders. Agile leaders need to guide by asking questions, not giving orders. This often calls for a huge cultural shift in command-and-control organisations, unaccustomed to cross-functional teams, shared goals and an innovation culture.[7]

Building a culture of innovation

The importance of the appropriate culture for innovation is also captured in a theory of organisational evolution pioneered by Frederic Laloux, a Belgian management thinker now working in the United States.[8] He observed that some teams unlock and amplify human potential better than others. These teams show three distinct characteristics compared with more traditional, common team structures.

1. They abandon formal hierarchies of leadership. Instead, leaders will emerge fluidly from the group and change as needed, depending on the project based on their expertise and ambition. Top-down hierarchies disappear. Their peers make them accountable for success and failure.

2. Work and personal life merge, as people come to perceive their identity in a singular holistic fashion as individuals with ambition, passion and caring, inclusive of both family and job. There is no work–life balance and no separation between company time and personal time as individuals bring their personal strengths and concerns into the company, and the company addresses each person's concerns.

3. According to Laloux, companies will recognise their social purpose in the world and redefine their mission away from purely market success towards solving a global problem. Profit will emerge from purposeful work that benefits the world. Laloux contends that this emphasis on social purpose, far from draining coffers, taps new sources of profits to create lucrative, mutually beneficial relationships between companies and customers that transcends transactions.

Laloux's ideal for organisational innovation seems utopian: a fantasy that could not exist in reality and might not deliver on its claims even if it were somehow to come into existence. We mention it here to show that innovative cultures do not necessarily exist only for the sake of creating new, impactful products and services. These company values, ethics and operating rules – and expectations – can be designed and implemented for the sake of the people who work in these institutions such that they feel a higher purpose. To bring this back to the agile approach to innovation, people on agile teams are not only more likely to generate creative ideas that solve customer problems. They are also more likely to have meaningful relationships with their co-workers, to feel as though they are using more of their human potential, and to remain engaged with the company's mission.

Dynamic capabilities

The concept of the three horizons asks organisations to develop multiple innovations, each at a different stage of development. Ambidexterity reminds organisations that, even if sales of their existing products are going well or they elect to shift towards innovation, they must accomplish both tasks at the same time. Agility offers some advice on how organisations can empower teams to shift between exploitation and exploration more efficiently and effectively.

All three pieces of advice for organisations to establish a culture and context for innovation fit within a single overarching theory called "dynamic capabilities". In 1997, economist and author David Teece recognised that, in rapidly changing markets, the winners were not companies with the most assets or brand reputation.[9] Instead, the winners were companies that had the processes, structure and culture to repeatedly follow a recipe for sensing new opportunities in the near and distant future, seizing those opportunities, and then reconfiguring the people and tasks within the company to scale their solutions.

This observation is consistent with the concepts of horizons, ambidexterity and agility. In fact, this theory embraces and ties these concepts together. Developing the capability for repeatedly sensing shifts in markets requires a different set of talents to those typically employed in most organisations. Sensing requires that people proactively anticipate and probe market trends and competitors, assessing new technologies and materials for their potential applicability to product innovations. Sensing also requires that companies develop the skills to rapidly seek, interpret and act on customer feedback. Sensing involves building hypotheses, what-if scenarios and prototypes of products that can be tested with real customers. (We will discuss these specific actions in later chapters.)

The capabilities for seizing involve the flexibility to change

Innovating with Impact

priorities on the fly, move resources and talent to where they are needed, and shift capital to fund new investments that are necessary to support the innovation. Organisations also need to have good relationships with suppliers and distributors who will be willing to assist in the quick transitions. Employees may be required to learn new skills or switch jobs or locations.

The third group of capabilities is the most difficult. As companies find and develop profitable innovations, they must transform themselves to exploit those innovations at scale, especially if competitors have yet to imitate the product or service. Highly successful radical innovations may mean that the company's core businesses and strategic planning need to evolve, requiring new policies, procedures and agreements with employees, suppliers and distributors.

Teece's three domains of dynamic capabilities set out critical guidelines for organisational leaders who are committed to sustainable innovation. Consider the case of Raden, the first significant company in the "smart suitcase" business. Founded in 2015 by Josh Udashkin, the company sensed that the luggage industry was ignoring the use of technology that could make suitcases much smarter. It seized on the opportunity to build batteries and tracking technology into suitcases so travellers could locate their luggage and recharge their mobile phones with it. Where the company failed, however, was in not managing to maintain the capabilities to dominate the competition. It had insufficient inventory to keep up with the demand, and distribution channels gave up, switching to competitors like Away. Raden went bankrupt in 2018.

This theory of dynamic capabilities has now received more than two decades of refinement. Many of the specific

44

recommendations that follow in the subsequent chapters have emerged from this seminal concept. At its core, this theory of innovation asks organisations to establish a consistent context – a company culture – that empowers innovative individuals to work together to find new, impactful ways to solve customer problems.

Open innovation

In the 16th and 17th centuries, the most powerful seafaring nations of Europe – Spain, the Netherlands, France, England, Portugal and the Venetian Republic – were competing aggressively to dominate global exploration and the overseas trade routes in search of gold, spices and textiles. Ship design and construction improved rapidly, as did ocean navigation. Many of these nations realised that whoever found the solution to the problem of tracking longitude was likely to become the winner of the trade wars. To incentivise the brilliant scientists and problem-solvers of the time several governments began offering substantial prize money for the winner of the competition. Thus began perhaps one of the earliest forms of what is now called "open innovation": inviting external stakeholders and contributors to innovate for you.

Through the turn of the millennium, many companies assumed that one of the vital roles of the firm was to come up with good ideas for new products. After all, this is what the corporate R&D department is for. It would have seemed absurd for Thomas Edison to envision the light bulb and then ask other people to work out how to make it.

The rise of open, efficient forms of two-way communication – most importantly the internet – allows companies to rethink that assumption. Companies now realise that not all the intelligence for a specific area of innovation lies inside the company's own building; there are clever people elsewhere who might like to help. The internet not only provides a useful way to communicate with innovators outside the firm's hallways, but also offers new ways for companies to generate profit from new ideas, even if they were created outside the company.

Organisations now rely on open innovation for a variety of reasons: to reduce their own R&D costs; to speed up product development; to identify and acquire new knowledge, intellectual property or talent; to reduce risk; to invest in a potential winning start-up; or to increase their differentiation among competitors in their markets.

Open innovation in practice

Successful examples of open innovation abound. The Danish company Lego launched a website to ask fans to submit ideas for new product designs using its traditional toy bricks. The company posts these new ideas for feedback. Once an idea reaches 10,000 supportive votes, Lego designers work with the idea's creator to design and manufacture a saleable product.

One of the fastest growing athletic apparel and footwear companies, Under Armour, sponsors an annual competition that invites inventors anywhere in the world to submit product ideas. The company receives 5,000–6,000 entries a year and selects about 10–15 inventors to come to its headquarters in Baltimore, MD to present their product at the company's Future Show held each October. Employees judge the products and select a winner who receives both a cash prize and an invitation to join the Under Armour product line.

Skin care company Nivea asked customers, through social media, to suggest ways to improve its deodorant. Users explained that the product stained their clothes. They also identified common household remedies to remove the stains.

Open innovation has spawned two dramatic shifts in the process of innovation. The first, as described above, is the realisation that an innovative company can find new ideas outside the company. These ideas can be found through crowdsourcing (asking a large audience for their opinions), competitions and acquisitions.

The second shift is based on the realisation that a company with a good idea does not necessarily have to commercialise the idea itself. It can find another company with an attitude and strategy of open innovation to purchase or license the idea. This is a core idea behind university-funded laboratories: they sell inventions to private companies, which transform them into scalable, valuable, impactful innovations. An example of this is the waterproof and breathable fabric GoreTex that W.L. Gore developed for a range of outdoor activities. The company produces and sells a wide range of its own clothing, but also licenses the GoreTex fabric technology and brand to scores of other companies that use it to produce shoes, clothing and medical products.

Netflix sponsored a crowdsourced competition in 2009 whose single winner netted a whopping $1m. The challenge was to invent a filtering algorithm that would predict user ratings on films based on how that user rated other films. No background information was provided about the user, only the past ratings. The winning team had to improve upon Netflix's own algorithm. Despite the expertise required to solve this problem, more than 40,000 teams from 186 countries entered the competition.

The open innovation strategy has fostered its own specialists. Quirky is a website devoted to helping amateur inventors see their product made and distributed. Anyone can submit an invention to the company, describing it as best they can and providing drawings as needed. The company then selects the top inventions submitted each month and works with the inventor to polish the design, take the product into prototyping and testing, and, if successful, arrange for its manufacturing and distribution. Winners receive a small percentage of the wholesale price of the invention.

What this means for you, for any of us, is that innovation is not only a team sport, but a cross-team sport. You can find opportunities in innovating with others, for others, and perhaps even taking innovative ideas from others.

Some companies solicit ideas through open innovation and then continue to develop those ideas inside the company through in-house incubators. For example, Shell initiated its GameChanger programme to work with and support start-ups on disruptive innovations in the energy field. Using their knowledge, resources, infrastructure and expertise, companies like Shell partner with promising start-ups, giving them everything from office space, mentoring and coaching through to help with strategy and business plans, introductions to networking partners and sales channels and help with navigating government regulation. In exchange, start-ups offer their host the potential for innovative ideas and/or products and, in some instances, the early rights to acquire them or own a substantial share if they succeed.

That does not mean that these so-called corporate incubators have been a wholehearted success.[10] Some fail because of misaligned goals between the host company and its start-ups, different expectations of growth rates and speed, or a cultural mismatch between the leadership of the host and that of the start-up. There are some important things to bear in mind for innovators who want to embrace a strategy of openness through incubators or competitions. These tactics require processes, policies, rules, guidelines, constraints, targets and metrics. They also require staff who are familiar with the balance between unfettered creativity and precise product specification. And they require a corporate culture that can accept ideas that were not invented inside the company's own buildings by people who are not on the company's payroll.

Large and nimble by design

In much of the work we do, we see two common struggles: those of start-ups looking to grow and become large established corporations; and the converse – large established corporations who want to remain nimble like budding start-ups. The 21st century is the century of the small entrepreneurial venture, sometimes moving fast and breaking things, often creating innovative products that take market share away from colossal incumbents and even force them out of business, as happened to Kodak.

Large organisations cannot easily act like scrappy start-ups. The good news is they don't need to. They can develop a culture that supports innovation through the elements identified in this chapter: a perspective on three horizons, appreciation of the need for ambidexterity, adoption of agile approaches and structures, and embracing open innovation. Besides, they can leverage their unique advantages to maintain and improve their position. In doing so, they must remain vigilant to the threats of overlooked but potentially disruptive innovations, and seize them before someone else does. This is the topic of the next chapter.

PART 2

Processes, tools and methods for innovation

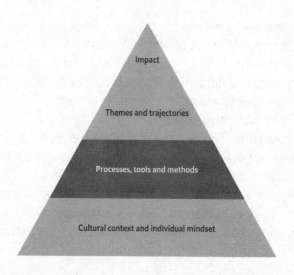

In Part 1, we built the foundation for the pyramid. We discussed what the individuals and organisations that succeed at innovating have in common. It is time now to explore what innovators do. How do they innovate? Are there any blueprints everyone can follow?

Indeed there are. Successful innovators adopt systematic and effective processes, tools and methods. You can too. This may seem contradictory. Isn't doing what others do the very opposite of innovation? On the surface, perhaps. We said innovation is about unlocking new value. These methods may not be innovative, but the impact will be.

How can a consistent recipe result in something unexpected, novel and impactful? Because the ingredients, combinations, sequences, circumstances and goals of each instance change, yielding different products and services.

This part of the book can be used by all types of individuals

– even those who do not have an innovative mindset or who work on teams without an innovative culture. By employing these methods, in fact, individuals and teams increase the likelihood, frequency and impact of innovations, making these individuals and teams more innovative by definition.

Chapter 3 demystifies the notion that impactful innovation must invariably change the world. For sure, some do. Many others are less dramatic, but no less innovative or less valuable. The chapter provides insight into various types of innovation, from products that deliver small incremental improvements to radical and disruptive shifts in entire markets, even discussing innovations that are valuable because they are *inferior* to existing solutions, like the *laufmaschine* was inferior to the horse.

After eliminating the pressure coming from the misunderstanding that innovating must be revolutionary, in Chapter 4 we discuss where to find ideas for innovations, some of which may be counter-intuitive. Chapter 5 describes a method to determine which of these ideas is most likely to create customer value as well as how to improve and refine your ideas.

In this part, we invite you not to reinvent the wheel, but follow in the steps of successful innovators so that you can invent something much more valuable.

3

Innovation as disruption

Like many areas of business practice, innovation has its own theories that explain and predict its origins and impact. One of the most ambitious and famous is the theory of disruptive innovation from the late Clayton Christensen, a professor at Harvard Business School.[1] He sought to understand why large and profitable companies so often fail eventually. After all, they have a wealth of resources – capital, talent, brand, ambition and reputation among them. Once a company has created a single successful product and reaped the rewards of its success, it should theoretically be willing and able to apply these resources to envision and launch many new products. By this logic, Andrew Carnegie's steel company should not only have continued to dominate the US metal market but also should have leveraged its successes to dominate globally. It should have anticipated – or even invented – new mining and foundry techniques, from the mini-mill to 3D printing. And yet it did not.

Similarly, IBM's early inventions in computing should logically have allowed it to make the leap from mainframe to desktop to cloud computing. It might have hired Bill Gates to grow Microsoft inside the company, instead of eventually being humbled by a start-up that has gone on since the 1980s to dominate the desktop software market with its MS-DOS and Windows operating systems and its cloud computing services. Ford should have invented Uber inside its own walls. Hilton should have invented Airbnb as its own subsidiary. Nike could have created Toms Shoes. Or, even better, Frye, one of the oldest shoe companies in the United States, should have created the sneaker.

To help explain why large companies eventually succumb to start-ups, Christensen recognised four types of innovations:

- sustaining
- "low end" disruptive
- "new market" disruptive
- radical.

Sustaining innovation

Sustaining innovations make incremental changes that gradually increase the features and appeal of a product or service. These innovations are usually targeted at the company's top-tier customers who are willing to pay higher prices for the improvements and enhanced features. Sustaining, incremental innovation avoids risk because it is based on listening to customers and responding to their wants. Companies that embrace this type of innovation are market-oriented and disciplined in a deliberate search for small tweaks that will sustain sales while improving profit margins.

Consider, for example, the bicycle industry. In the 1960s, a bicycling boom began in both Europe and the United States as people started to recognise the health benefits of exercise. This attracted millions of new customers to biking. From about 1960 to 1980, the top manufacturers of bikes switched from making the heavier cruiser style bike with thick tyres and a heavy frame to more lightweight bikes with thin tyres and multiple gears. Year after year, incremental innovation took the traditional three-gear bike up to 10, 15 and 21 gears, some with dropped handlebars for racing rather than simply touring. Further sustaining innovations continued in bike design, with extremely lightweight carbon-fibre frames, smooth switching derailleur gears, and strong wheel hubs and spokes. All these improvements substantially raised the average prices of bikes, with customers willing to spend thousands rather than hundreds of dollars on a touring or racing bike.

In the 1980s, customers became interested in cycling off-pavement on dirt roads through mountains and forests, so the biking industry innovated yet again and began manufacturing mountain bikes with thick treaded tyres for better traction and suspension forks and seats to take the bumps of off-road biking. A mountain biking craze took off and poured millions of dollars of profit into bike manufacturers, retailers and speciality bike touring companies. In this century, the biking industry continues to create sustaining innovations through new styles of bikes such as hybrid bikes for use in commuting on city streets. Innovations include medium-width tyres, straight handlebars so the biker sits up to view traffic, hidden gears to prevent damage to exterior derailleurs, and sturdy but lightweight frames so that they can be carried into offices and apartments.

This pattern of constant improvement in features can be seen in nearly every industry, from home appliances, industrial machinery and automotive design to banking and car rental services. Sustaining innovations have two goals: to entice customers to return repeatedly to purchasing one's products or services, even at higher prices, by providing them with apparent greater value; and to lower the cost of production to increase profit margins.

Keep in mind that not every sustaining innovation succeeds. Many leading companies have launched an "improved" product only to find that customers reject the new design or features. The iPhone 12 mini is often touted as one of the least successful sustaining innovations in the entire iPhone history of successive models. Samsung's Galaxy Note 7 became a dangerous failure by virtue of its overheating that caused it to burst into flames; it was banned from air travel. Google's Allo app, the technology giant's attempt to defend its dominance of everything technology against the upstart WhatsApp, was such a failure that it was withdrawn from the market within two years.

Low-end disruptive innovation

Christensen juxtaposed the gradualism of sustaining innovations with a form of innovation he recognised as an increasingly common pattern. He called this process "disruptive innovation" as the outcome of such innovation disrupts the market dominance of incumbents. The process often, but not always, initiates when the dominant players in a market demonstrate little interest in fulfilling the needs of customers at the lowest end of profitability. Their products or services and constant sustaining innovations require increasingly higher prices that some customers cannot afford and thus stop purchasing from that company. Even a low-risk opportunity is deemed unattractive if success would result in only a trivial uptick in revenue. This leads companies intentionally to neglect opportunities with low margins to attract the "poorer" customers. Even if the company were able to adapt one of its products to serve these customers, they would contribute negligible profits.

This leaves an opening for entrepreneurial firms to exploit. If an upstart company can find a way to entice non-consumers to consume a similar "good enough" product or service at a lesser price, they can capture a piece of that market for themselves, in plain view of the larger incumbents. Christensen pointed out that technology – the use of the internet or an app – is often the enabler that allows disruptive entrepreneurs to create advantages for consumers, by making the product or service simpler to use, easier to access, and more affordable because the firm can lower the costs of manufacturing and/or distribution.

In this way, disruptive start-ups manage to grab a small foothold in the market. The incumbents do not usually feel threatened as they remain focused on their higher-end customers. However, the disruption intensifies as the start-ups reap in cash from early profits and continue to improve their version of the product or service, still with lower costs and higher profitability. The entrepreneurial company then slowly marches upmarket, attracting segments of the incumbent's customers who are seeking greater value. At some point, the shock becomes apparent and the start-up's disruption becomes complete as its products or services attract even the top-tier customers in that market. The disrupter becomes the new dominant player in the industry. This is the pattern that

Christensen recognised as the process by which many notable incumbents lost their stature and profitability.

A classic example of low-end disruptive innovation is Netflix versus Blockbuster. Founded in 1997, Netflix launched its film subscription service using the internet to reach consumers who preferred lower prices to rent DVDs and receive them by post rather than pay the higher prices at video rental stores like Blockbuster. Netflix's core market initially differed from Blockbuster's, as its customers were less interested in renting new films than simply having a decent inventory of films to rent at cheap pricing. As the market leader, Blockbuster had thousands of retail stores and millions of customers who wanted to browse the inventory and rent these most recent films, so did not recognise the need to compete with Netflix's appeal to consumers on price, convenience and a good-enough product selection.

But as Netflix gained millions of subscribers over the years, it used its profits to develop the technology to deliver a streaming service, making the DVDs themselves redundant, let alone physical stores. With a larger subscriber base, Netflix also gained the clout to negotiate with Hollywood distributors to release their new films immediately after the theatrical runs. By 2010, Blockbuster declared bankruptcy, unable to compete with Netflix's mushrooming market dominance based on its ability to provide customers with far greater value in accessing entertainment. Netflix is now not only a leading purveyor of Hollywood entertainment but a major producer of its own films and TV shows as well.

Nearly every industry has seen disruptive innovation shake up its list of incumbent firms. In the steel industry, mini-mills offering far lower costs for specialised products have eaten away at the revenues of the largest steel companies. In the mortgage business, dozens of entrepreneurial firms have encroached on the former big bank leaders using technology to make mortgage loans and closing costs more affordable.

New market disruptive innovation

Christensen outlined a third pattern in which disruptive innovation is used to open up an entirely new market for a product or service. Whereas the disruptive pattern based on affordability is focused on attracting new consumers to an existing market, *new market disruption* is focused on bringing in entirely new consumers who were not able to use a product or service before.

The market for electricity in rural undeveloped economies illustrates the success of this path. These markets are dominated by a few large traditional utilities in each country that generate energy from large hydroelectric or fossil-fuel plants and then deliver electricity through an expensive infrastructure of high-voltage electrical wires on elevated electrical poles. This approach to generating and distributing electricity is efficient when serving large amounts of electricity to customers in close proximity to each other. However, it leaves out of the market more than 700 million people in the world who live in very rural areas and whose income is typically less than $2 a day who have no options for lighting their homes at night.

The founders of Angaza created a solution for such customers. Recognising that purchasing even a small, portable solar lantern is prohibitively expensive for these rural customers, and that their extremely low incomes disincline any bank to offer them credit, Angaza built a solar lantern business that allows such consumers to pay for hours of light with their cellular telephone when they have the funds. The company sells them the lantern at marginal cost and earns most of its revenues and profits through the purchases of light. The company has since worked with manufacturers to incorporate its low-tech payment solution into other products for impoverished consumers in Africa, South America and Southeast Asia. As it expands its share and scope, Angaza may soon also attract customers within the traditional electrical system with a more flexible efficient way to light dark corners.

New market disruption is not always about a product or service; it can also occur in a company's approach to marketing and sales. Consider Solar Sister, which also sells solar lanterns in rural sub-Saharan Africa. Its founder, Katherine Lucey, recognised that it is the woman of the household who is traditionally tasked with procuring fuel or kindling for the fire to light the house after dark. So the woman of the house is the person most likely to understand the value of an alternative lighting source. To create the new market disruption needed to sell its solar lanterns, Solar Sister decided to employ exclusively women in its sales force. Women salespeople have more credibility and connection with household matriarchs. This new market innovation taps into an existing, under-used resource – entrepreneurial women – to create a new way to bring value to its customers.

The debate: was Uber a disruptive innovation?

Whether Uber should be considered one of the most significant disrupting innovations is a debate that has found proponents on both sides. In an article in the *Harvard Business Review*,² Christensen insisted that Uber is not a disruptive innovation to the taxi industry because it targeted neither affordability nor expanded utility as its core business model. He believes most taxi customers were not looking for good-enough cheaper rides, nor did Uber target people who had not used taxis before. To Christensen, having either a low-end or unserved customer strategy is a requisite to being a disruptive innovator, as it impacts how a company creates its business model, target market, pricing and long-range strategic planning to take over a market. In his view, all Uber did was to enlarge the market for people seeking to rent rides by making finding rides easier, faster and more convenient using Uber's app and technology for payment.

Other innovation theorists argue that Uber is nevertheless a good example of disruptive innovation. Uber journeys were generally more affordable than taxis, and the ease of use of the Uber app and rapid response from thousands of Uber drivers appealed to people who were looking for a good enough alternative to phoning and waiting for a taxi to appear. They also point out that Uber originally started as an affordable alternative to limousine services and disrupted that industry by offering good enough black cars. The company then moved upmarket by allowing black-car renters to reserve up to 30 days in advance, just as a limousine company allowed.

Companies like Uber, Lyft, Ola and BlaBlaCar have also disrupted more than the limousine and taxi industries. The radical innovation of ride hailing also provides a less expensive, more convenient alternative to owning a car, to the extent that the entire automotive industry has been affected. The growth of services like Uber Pool, which fills cars with multiple passengers, has precipitated a decline in the demand to purchase new vehicles.

Whichever side of the debate you might be on, the key is that Christensen's two-pronged patterns of disruptive innovation are critical guidelines for any company looking for the right model to follow if they intend to overtake dominant incumbents. There may be grey areas in the definition of what constitutes affordability, or a satisfactory product or service, or which consumers are a new market, but the overall patterns still appear to hold true among successful disruptive entrepreneurial firms.

Radical innovation

Christensen's primary focus was on recognising how entrepreneurial firms increasingly pursue the model of disruptive innovation to march upmarket and topple leading companies that fail to pay attention to all segments of their market. These innovations do not rely on scientific or technological breakthroughs. They are more often innovations in how value is created or delivered to the customer.

Christensen, of course, recognised that formal research and development could also generate "radical" innovations. Pharmaceutical companies, for example, spend years and millions of dollars to find radically new products using new technologies, materials or formulas that their teams invent and that completely alter the landscape of an existing field of products. Radical innovation is not about affordability, as the innovations typically enter the marketplace at very high price ranges to compensate the company for the large investment it had to make in creating the new product.

The Toyota Prius launched in 1997 is an example of radical innovation in hybrid car technology, followed in 2004 by Elon Musk and his company Tesla's radical innovation to create a reliable long-range all-electric car. Several companies are now leading the radical innovation of self-driving cars, including Google, Uber, AutoX, Arity, Optimus Ride and others.

Radical innovation is typically the domain of wealthy companies with large R&D departments full of scientists, engineers and technology specialists who can spend millions or hundreds of millions over many years to make the discoveries needed to alter the status quo in a given product field. The leading companies in every industrial field, from computer chip manufacturing to farm equipment to chemicals to making roofing materials and paint, all invest in deep R&D with the expectation of creating not just a sustaining innovation but often a radical one that might gain them a superior position over their competitors.

The problem with radical innovation is that no one can be certain of the pay-off. Companies do their best to research the need for the radical innovation, so some radical leaps reach new heights of customer delight, solving problems in entirely new ways, resulting in gains in market share, revenue growth and profitability, and in some cases toppling the market dominance of the established leaders. But if customer demand is lacking, such innovation leaps end in ignominious failure.

A perfect example of a radical innovation failure is the case of the Segway electric two-wheel vehicle. Invented by Dean Kamen and launched in 2001, the Segway PT was supposed to be a breakthrough in how people would transport themselves through and around cities for commuting and pleasure. The device was intended to be easy to operate with its self-balancing mechanism that took years to develop. Anyone was supposed to be able to stand on a Segway and roll forwards or backwards with speeds up to 12mph.

Nevertheless, despite the hype, Segway generated lacklustre interest among consumers, who perceived it as being gawky, unsafe, too slow to offer meaningful transportation, and too expensive at its original purchase price of about $5,000, for which one could buy a faster and much more useful scooter or motorcycle. In addition to the severe consumer disinterest, many cities outlawed Segways on sidewalks for pedestrian safety reasons and provided no parking areas for them. All in all,

Segway Inc. floundered in its sales projections, achieving only 1% of its target in the first seven years. In 2015, the company was sold to Ninebot, which decided to halt all production of the Segway PT in July 2020.

However, the failure of Segway might be considered to have led to the disruptive innovation in the people transportation field that has recently stormed cities throughout the world – electric scooters. Companies like Bird and Spin (acquired by Ford Motor Company and then Tier Mobility) applied the developing technology of powerful, long-lasting battery-powered miniaturised motors to transform urban commuting with far greater success than Segway. Scooters easily overcame consumer concerns over safety and awkwardness because the transporters are low to the ground, easy to steer and stop, and quick to learn how to use, effectively tapping into everyone's childhood memory of a foot-powered scooter. Within a few months of Bird and Spin arriving on the scene, cities around the world had thousands of scooters standing available on every corner, ready for consumers to rent by the minute at cheap rates and then leave at their destination. Cities have generally tolerated the lack of parking regulations, allowing scooters to be left curbside.

Scooter companies have also innovated to solve the problem of how to recharge their scooters cost-effectively. Bringing all the scooters into a central facility would reduce their availability throughout a city. Building hundreds of recharging stations throughout a city would be both cost-prohibitive and potentially inconvenient for customers. Instead, the companies typically pay homeowners in a city to bring nearby scooters inside their own homes to recharge and then put the scooter back onto the street when its battery is full. They are thus tapping into under-used assets – electrical capacity inside of homes – to provide a solution that offers urban residents an affordable method of transportation.

Disruptive innovation in action

We can look at the effects of disruptive innovation through the example of the waves of digital innovation we've experienced since the 1990s. Back then, enabled by a new way of accessing information and therefore of conducting business, early digital ventures began by offering customers the chance to access *only* the *specific* content they wanted. Once upon a time, people bought newspapers, which offered a bundle of content: primarily news, but also op-eds, classified ads, weather forecasts and book reviews, to name but a few. But the internet made it possible to break down such bundles into their individual components and to distribute them individually. Google unbundled articles. Yelp unbundled the restaurant reviews. Craigslist unbundled the classified ads. Apple's iTunes unbundled songs from albums. Disrupted incumbents rapidly experienced substantial losses.

Thales Teixeira of Harvard Business School has identified this *unbundling* of content as the first wave of digital disruption.[3] The most recent manifestation of this wave is the unbundling of entire business models. For example, banks have traditionally operated complex business models based on numerous services: accounts, payments, loans and investments. Fintech start-ups entered the market with unbundled services.[4] In the United States, for example, Credit Karma offered credit scoring; UK's Wise (formerly TransferWise) offered international money transfer; China's Lufax offered peer-to-peer lending. Even as incumbent banks prepared to respond, fintechs then launched a counter-wave, expanding their offerings by effectively re-bundling the business model: Credit Karma introduced tax preparation services, and Lufax introduced wealth management and credit rating.

In the early 2000s, a second wave of digital disruption emerged: *disintermediation*. Digital players broke down supply chains and went directly to consumers leaving behind the middlemen. Low-cost airline Easyjet, for example, sold tickets directly to passengers, cutting out travel agents. Amazon cut out the express couriers by delivering goods directly to its customers. Once again, incumbents suffered. Travel agencies are now pretty much a thing of the past. This wave peaked in the early 2000s, but digital technology is now empowering a counter-wave: re-intermediation. For example, Amazon offers the services of an express courier to other companies, and companies such as Deliveroo and Uber Eats act as an intermediary between restaurants and customers.

Decoupling, the third and latest wave of digital disruption, is the breaking down of the customer value chain. Consumer activities that have traditionally been done together or in sequence are now separated. Some players focus on only one of these activities or have improved it so much that they transformed the customer's experience. When customers want new cosmetics, they may go to a shop like Sephora, explore the available offerings, try them, choose the ones they like, purchase and take them home, then use them several times and eventually dispose of them. Some companies are decoupling this value chain. For example, Birchbox is a subscription service that sends sample cosmetics to customers, making sampling them easy. In other words, it does not sell cosmetics; it focuses on the sampling stage of the value chain. Zipcar makes driving a car easy, by decoupling it from buying and maintaining one. Kayak and Skyscanner make comparing flights easy. Dollar Shave Club makes restocking razorblades easy via its monthly subscription. By focusing on only one stage of the customer value chain, these organisations can offer substantial cost savings for customers.

The opportunities for decoupling are endless. The ultimate example is Trov, an insurance company that offers on-demand coverage for individual items and for custom duration. For example, you can insure your digital camera for a weekend trip without buying the full annual policy. Wherever there is an inefficient process or a wasteful service, there is an opportunity to decouple.

Lessons of disruptive innovation

Why should you care about Christensen's theory of disruptive innovation? There are three key lessons to take from it.

1. Not all innovation has to aim to topple corporate behemoths. Smaller ideas aimed at incremental improvements to existing products help companies to sustain their profit margins and competitive edge.

2. The theory gives aspiring innovators a commonly overlooked locus for finding impactful new ways to generate customer value: low-end innovations that bring new customers into a market by offering more affordable options. This observation allows innovators to avoid

"bigger and better" product features to focus instead on "smaller and cheaper".

3. It warns incumbents in an industry that, even if they know about entrepreneurial orientation, ambidexterity or dynamic capabilities, they will probably succumb to a new entrant's disruptive innovation because these upstarts nibble away at the edges of its markets. Not every entrepreneurial competitor can develop a good enough product or service that has the strength to grow on and march upmarket. Incumbents need to scan the horizon for new competitors whose products or services have features that could eventually beat their products or services.

The theory of disruptive innovation gives us some general advice to categorise different types of innovations. However, its critics accuse the theory of being overly general. They say that it can tell us what kind of innovations typically work, but does not tell us precisely where to look for the ideas that might eventually become disruptive. Nor, they complain, does this theory give us repeatable processes to determine whether a new idea will be valuable to customers. Our next step is to be even more specific about where to find unmet customer needs. The next chapter gives us several different options.

4

Innovation as a process

Competition among supermarket chains and independents is fierce. They compete extensively on food pricing, product quality, product uniqueness and convenience for consumers. The "switching cost" of consumers jumping from one chain to another is low: to a large extent, the same or similar grocery items are available in nearly every store. The supermarkets compete on price such that discounted prices on a group of items in one chain for one week are likely to be similar in a competing chain the next week. And there are new entrants into the market: increasingly, consumers can shop for groceries at local mini-markets, petrol stations and even former retail stores like Target, which has introduced a grocery section.

Assume you work in the retail grocery industry for one of the chains and you want to innovate to obtain an additional competitive advantage. The company is already highly experienced in sustaining innovations, having implemented many improvements such as more attractive shelving, better shopping trolleys and a greater selection of prepared foods. The company's history, existing profile and brand strength do not support the need for low-end disruptive innovation. So how might you accomplish some other type of innovation that will add value for customers?

This chapter discusses three other approaches to innovation: ethnography, design thinking and blue ocean strategy. All three have become successful methods and have been used in companies of all sizes. What distinguishes them is that they all focus on *finding and meeting unmet customer needs in order to create a new market*.

These three methods share two additional assumptions that merit their inclusion in this chapter.

1. They assume that the innovator is not trying to improve on or counteract the features of a competing product. In other words, these methods promote a deep inquiry into customer problems for the sake of solving those problems, such that competition is a secondary motive.

2. They assume that the problems that customers face are not immediately obvious. Perhaps the customers do not even know that a problem exists – or that a circumstance in their lives could be improved – until an innovator shows them how their lives could be better.

Ethnography

Ethnography has been used for decades as a fundamental qualitative market research technique to get to know one's customers and deeply understand their habits, expectations and challenges. The process involves becoming a neutral and silent observer of customers as they go about their daily lives. The focus is on observing the customer's social behaviours, not on soliciting their opinions through surveys or interviews. Innovators want to know what customers *actually* do, not what they think they do or what they think they want.

For example, if you wanted to support innovation in the grocery shopping sector with an ethnographic study to assess customer experience, you would follow a process such as that outlined below.

1. The customer experience begins in the car park, so you might find a position behind a car where you are unnoticed in order to watch how customers park their cars and enter the supermarket. Are they in a rush? Do they know which door to go through? Do they try to find a trolley in the car park? Do they look in their pockets or purses to find their coupons? Do most customers shop alone or with children or others in tow?

2. After spending some time assessing customer behaviour outside the supermarket, you might go inside, continuing to be an unnoticed observer of shopping behaviours. Did the customers obtain a shopping trolley or basket easily? Do most of them head towards a specific area first? Do customers appear to know where to go? Do they look at the signage to find what they need? Do they appear confused or lost, walking from aisle to aisle? Do they seem impatient to find a specific item, walking quickly and forcefully towards a specific spot? Or are they happy to meander, considering impulse purchases or thinking ahead to next week's grocery needs as they walk?

3. If there is music playing in the background, do customers appear to enjoy it or are they annoyed by it? Are they tapping their toes to the music or trying to talk above it or issuing mean glances towards the nearest stereo speaker? As customers fill their shopping trolley, do they need to constantly move items around to prevent fragile items

from being crushed by heavier items? Do customers leave their trolley in one area while they fetch products in other aisles or do they push it in a clear sequence of aisles? At the checkout, do they appear impatient or in a hurry, even if they were not in a hurry while shopping?

An ethnographic study usually takes place without subjective opinions from the observer or immediate discussions with the customers (although, as we'll see below, there are variations of ethnography that allow for the boundaries between observer and subject to be erased through follow-on interviews, surveys and other direct contact). The results from a well-performed study can help innovators deconstruct the customer experience and recognise problems that can be solved through innovative thinking. Because it is cost-effective, ethnography is often the first step in an innovation process

If this study concluded that a large share of customers do not need a shopping trolley but prefer a basket, the supermarket might introduce a conveyor belt mechanism outside the store that delivers clean, washed baskets to the customer at the entrance. If customers are looking primarily for discount items, a digital sign might be installed at the entrance displaying the main price reductions that day. If customers seem to be lost and cannot find the products in the aisles, digital signage might be projected onto the floors in each aisle, making it easier to find products rather than by looking up at small signs hung above the aisles. If the supermarket has a busy period right before dinner time, an innovation might be to have a specialised dinner section with pre-prepared foods and common dinner-time products in one section to speed up the customer's shopping time.

Ethnography studies encourage innovators to fall in love

with the problems they uncover, before the innovator falls in love with one particular solution. Observing consumers first-hand in the act of using a product requires objectivity, as discussed in Chapter 1. The innovator can literally see how the customer struggles with something.

Design thinking

Design thinking goes beyond ethnography to explore the human dynamics and the systemic context of problems. A leading company that uses design thinking, defines it as follows: "As long as you stay focused on the people you're designing for – and listen to them directly – you can arrive at optimal solutions that meet their needs."

Design thinking's arrival into the field of innovation is primarily attributed to David Kelley, the founder of IDEO (pronounced EYE-dee-oh), a consulting firm dedicated to solving customer problems. Kelley started out with a BA degree in electrical engineering and worked at Boeing where he designed the "Lavatory occupied" sign for the 747 aircraft. This sign – with its icons, colours and placement – enables passengers to see from far away whether to approach the toilet on a plane, even if they do not speak a common language.

Design thinking is defined by a mindset and a process, and it relies on a large toolkit that can be selectively used depending on circumstances.[1] The design thinking mindset is human-centred, or geared towards understanding the people involved and listening to their feedback, and built on broad collaborations, by bringing together individuals with different perspectives and backgrounds, because diversity engenders creativity and insight. Despite its name, the focus of this approach is not on thinking, but doing: experimenting, learning by trial and error and building preliminary prototypes are all integral to design thinking.

The process rests on five sequential steps, but should not be mistaken for a linear methodology. It is an iterative and recursive methodology that affords ever-improving results as it is repeated.

1. **Empathise**. The first step consists in understanding the user or the customer for whom you intend to solve a problem or create value, by empathising with them. The problems you're trying to solve are generally not your own but someone else's, usually a customer or user. Therefore you must understand them and what matters to them. This works best when you set aside any preconceptions and conduct research to gain authentic insight.

Effective interviews with the Mom Test

The Mom Test method derives its name from the idea that you should never ask your mother if your business idea is good. She loves you. So she will say yes irrespective of its merits. Similarly, most prospective customers will *say* they'd buy your product, if you push them enough. It does not mean they *will*. So, the Mom Test is a set of principles to conduct effective client interviews so that even your mother will give you useful insights. You should always ask questions that result in factual information and not generic opinions.

Rob Fitzpatrick, the author of this method, recommends talking about your customers' life instead of your idea, asking about specifics and examples in the past instead of generics or opinions about the future and, above all, talking less and listening more. Ultimately, your purpose is not to pitch an idea that is still raw, but to uncover insights about your customers' concerns, desires, goals, constraints and problems.[2]

Ethnographic research, as discussed above, is a great way to empathise. Another effective technique is talking to users or interviewing them. Engaging and connecting with people uncovers their thoughts and values, especially those they hold tacitly, and can be a powerful way to unlock unexpected insights. In the introduction to this book, we gave the example of skyscrapers' residents hating lifts because they were too slow. Through empathy, we could discover that the problem was not the speed of the elevators, but the wait.

2. **Define**. The second step is a synthesis of the findings from the first step. The definition step extracts your deep understanding of the users and the context, and consolidates them into a rigorous but actionable problem statement. Ultimately, you need to be able to express what is the outcome your user strives for and why. Such clarity is critical. Reframing the problem definition is an essential step towards finding a valuable solution. This is the difference between "making lifts faster" and "making the wait less frustrating". This is also the difference between a technical solution based on assumptions and a human-centred solution based on empathy.

Uncovering your customer's job to be done

With the expansion of the internet, newspaper sales started dropping. An interesting way of looking at this phenomenon is that people never wanted newspapers in the first place. They wanted to be informed in order to make better decisions and to look intelligent and up to date while chatting with their peers. When newspapers were the best way to achieve this, people bought them. When the internet offered a richer, more timely and cheaper solution, newspaper companies began to fold. It was not a better newspaper that put them out of business, but a better way of helping readers achieve their goals.

The jobs-to-be-done theory is based on the notion that customers do not buy products and services for their own sake, but because they need to get some "job" done.[3] A marketing professor from Harvard Business School, Theodore Levitt, said: "People don't want to buy a quarter-inch drill. They want a quarter-inch hole." His quotation was often referenced by the late Clayton Christensen, another Harvard professor and key proponent of the jobs-to-be-done theory.

One way to understand your customers and their problems is to focus on the drill. What is it used for, how often, for how many holes, in what context? Some improved drills now have batteries and so can be used away from a power socket, giving users more freedom. Some feature an LED light on the tip, to illuminate the work area. But this is just the beginning. Indeed, most people don't want drills, but holes. Why do they need holes? Where? What for? 3M has answered these questions and developed adhesive hooks for those customers who want a drill to make a hole to hang a picture. It turns out that, for many users, an expensive drill can be replaced with an inexpensive adhesive hook. Focusing on the job instead of the product liberates you to generate better solutions to get your customer's job done effectively.

Jobs have functional and emotional aspects and each existing solution afford gains and imply pains. When Alessandro contemplates buying his first Ferrari, he intends to use it to drive from A to B, fast and in style (functional job). But he will not buy a Ferrari *just for that*. He will buy it because it will make him feel that he's succeeded (emotional job, or how one feels about oneself) and for the pleasure of driving up to a restaurant and attracting looks of excitement, envy or contempt (social job, or how others feel about someone). Until then, Alessandro will more responsibly ride his bike to work (functional job). This way he exercises and feels good about himself (emotional job). Moreover, he feels like he belongs in the group of cyclists (social job). If you uncover these aspects when defining the job to be done, you can create solutions that help users get their important jobs done, better, faster or more cheaply.

3. **Ideate**. When the problem definition is clear, most people intuitively jump to a conclusion for a viable solution. It is natural to think this way. Unfortunately, for most people, the first idea that comes to mind is seldom the best. Often it is the most obvious and it is rarely creative. We know this from both research and anecdotal evidence. One of our colleagues has developed a creativity exercise where students are sent to a breakout room with a design brief: draw the world as seen by a fly. When they come back, they excitedly start sharing their drawings. The excitement rapidly declines when they realise that almost everyone draws the same recurring tropes: a multi-faceted 360° world, large humans, trees and buildings, some food, whether appetising or not, and dangers. Less than 2% of the students offer something genuinely creative. To avoid this trap, you need to generate multiple ideas. On many occasions, abandoning your first idea is your best course of action. Generating numerous ideas increases the chances of one of them being high quality. Many famous techniques can help doing so: brainstorming, brain writing, de Bono's six thinking hats, SCAMPER (substitute, combine, adapt, modify/magnify, purpose, eliminate/minimise and rearrange/reverse an existing product to innovate it) and even crazy eights rapid sketching. Whatever tool you use to generate ideas, ideation sessions should help you find a new angle.

Crazy sketching for creativity

An effective method to accelerate creativity during the ideation stage is called crazy eights. It is a rapid sketching challenge to sketch eight totally distinct ideas in eight minutes. The purpose is to force participants to push beyond their initial idea and instead explore many possibilities. We mentioned that design thinking encourages collaboration. However, collaboration sometimes fails, for example when a particularly extrovert member dominates the discussion so that others progressively disengage or simply approve of everything the dominant member recommends. Anybody can have a great inspiration, but groupthink and other group dynamics sometimes cull inspiration.

To avoid this, crazy eights – like brain writing – is an individual task, where each member must sketch independently, with the proviso that each of the eight solutions must be profoundly different from the others. One way to encourage diversity is by requiring that one solution should be for Elon Musk, another should work even if users cannot talk, another should be free of cost, yet another should work in outer space. This is a powerful method to prompt creativity.

4. **Prototype**. Of the many ideas that potentially hold promise, only a handful will be viable. But you are rarely the best positioned to determine which one. Prospective users are better at this. Instead of ceaselessly talking about hypothetical variants or elements of your solution, you should develop a prototype to make your ideas accessible; for David Kelley of IDEO: "If a picture is worth 1,000 words, a prototype is worth 1,000 meetings." A prototype is not necessarily a preliminary version of the final product or solution. It is a mock-up that helps stakeholders understand the basic forms, uses or values of the solution. A prototype could be an online advertisement

with a simple tag line; if users click on it, that means it's attractive to them. You don't need to develop a whole e-commerce website. Then, if users don't find your offering attractive – and so don't click on the ad – you will not have wasted resources developing a website. There's a rule of thumb called 1–10–100. Prevention costs $1, correction costs $10, failure costs $100. A prototype is the $1 investment that potentially saves you $100. Prototypes can help you further empathise, define or ideate, but they are typically developed for the next step.

5. **Test**. The example of the digital ad above illustrates the final step of the design thinking process. Prototypes are developed to run tests with prospective users. Their feedback will be invaluable to avoid committing resources for a solution without future. Since 2014, the consulting firm CB Insights has been conducting research on hundreds of start-ups that have gone bankrupt.[4] The study reveals that one of the most common reasons why start-ups fail is that there is no market need for their offering. Running inexpensive tests with quick and dirty prototypes is a powerful way to mitigate such risk. (We discuss testing in greater detail in the next chapter.)

Design thinking in practice

Since its founding, IDEO has used design thinking to redesign thousands of products, processes, services and strategies in nearly every type of industry. The firm originally created the computer mouse for Steve Jobs to be used with Apple's Lisa computer, allowing a user to use their hand on a desktop to control a cursor on a screen in a way that is so intuitive that no training is required.

IDEO worked with General Electric to reimagine how a patient experiences a computerised axial tomography (CAT) scanner in a hospital. The patient must lie flat on a table, which is then inserted into the machine like a bun in an oven. The machine emits loud clicking noises. The entire experience is emotionally jarring. Using soft lighting, neutral colours and pleasant ambient sounds, the experience of having a CAT scan has been made more calming. In a later development, GE even made CAT and fMRI (functional magnetic resonance imaging) scans child-friendly. Using design thinking, GE decorated the rooms with stickers representing a tropical scene, and developed an adventurous story where the young patients enter a "pirate adventure". When the scan requires the child to lay still, the story is framed as the child needing to remain motionless so an evil pirate won't see them. When the scanner makes its loud noise, the story describes noises as cannon shots. In another experience, children are on a canoe, where they must stay still so as not to rock the boat and lie low as the projection of a fish jumps over the canoe.

In 1999, the US television programme *Nightline* commissioned IDEO to redesign a supermarket shopping trolley to show viewers how the process works. Designers at IDEO spent a day examining problems with the standard shopping trolley from a customer perspective. They noted that it was dangerous for infants and young children sitting in the child seat because it could tip over easily. The trolley was not easily manoeuverable because of its wheel design. Shoppers had no way of separating the various products they were buying as the trolley was simply one big basket. The standard trolley made checking out and holding the bags cumbersome and slow.

Within a single day, the team produced various prototype redesigns and then merged the leading ideas into a newly designed shopping trolley the next day. The human-centred shopping trolley had multiple baskets so shoppers could categorise their selections. It had its own scanner so consumers could scan their products and tally their spending before checking out. The trolley's wheels turned 90 degrees for easy manoeuvering in tight aisles and around other trolleys. It had hooks to hold the shopper's bags. And finally, the redesigned trolley would cost about the same as the traditional trolley, making it appealing to supermarkets.

After passively observing customers, the process of design thinking encourages an innovator to become more active, interviewing customers, owners, suppliers and employees to understand the benefits and constraints that they all face. Team members map the "ripples" in the product or service, exploring possible interconnections that might make an initially obvious solution not a good choice in the long run.

IDEO's work with PillPack offers another example of design thinking in action. The firm was founded in 2013 to improve the experience of people buying pharmaceutical medications. The founders and designers noted that millions of people must drive to a pharmacy to obtain their medications, must open a bottle that has a seal and childproof lid, must not confuse one pill with another, and must remember to take a specific pill at a specific time. They examined and reconceived every aspect of the experience, from ordering to delivery through to travelling with pills and asking questions of a pharmacist.

This exercise in human-centred design delivered the experience that customers had long sought: prescription medications delivered by post on a regular schedule to the patient's home. PillPack's business grew rapidly until it was purchased by Amazon in 2018 for $1 billion.

The challenges of design thinking

Design thinking is not without its flaws. Many firms find it too time consuming and cumbersome, and does not fit into their fast-paced culture. Their product development and marketing teams believe they already know their customers and their customers' problems, and thus do not need to be so rigorous. Other critics warn that design thinking searches for the ideal solution without considering solutions that might be "good enough".

Witness the Danish hearing aid manufacturer Oticon. After investigating customer problems, members of the company's design thinking team concluded that the design of contemporary hearing aids could be improved to deliver better auditory performance. However, other departments in the company were unprepared and unwilling to accept the feedback. The company culture was so antithetical to having a design team that the team was not provided with a physical space for meetings. Eventually, the other departments perceived the design team as disruptive of their work. The team was disbanded within three years, having produced nothing of value.[5]

Design thinking requires a laser focus on the customer experience. The process does not (intentionally) consider whether existing products might address customer problems. For example, it's possible that a small, mostly unknown company in a far corner of the planet has already built the perfect shopping trolley. Nor does design thinking consider if the ideal solution fits within the existing competencies and brand reputation of the sponsoring company. The conclusion of the exercise sponsored by PillPack might be more cheaply and effectively offered by Walmart than by Amazon. Consequently, the results of a process of design thinking might increase competition between firms, perhaps resulting in a price war or a turf battle that damages companies, suppliers and even customers.

Despite these challenges, design thinking provides a customer-centric process for innovators to create novel, valuable products and services. The recipe is especially useful for customer experiences that can be improved through iterative experimentation.

Blue ocean strategy

In 2005, two professors at INSEAD, France's top business school, Chan Kim and Renée Mauborgne, realised that innovative companies often launched products that both solved a customer problem and directly and intentionally bested a rival product, increasing competition in the industry.[6] This competition created "red oceans" full of the blood of competitors fighting each other for an ever-decreasing share of the market pie. They advised innovators to consider a different path: innovators who seek to occupy "blue oceans" of expansive uncrowded new territory that is as yet undiscovered by competitors.

To find new unoccupied markets, Kim and Mauborgne ask innovators to recombine the attributes of existing products, sometimes even removing features and raising prices to create a new product. The goal is to define and entice new customers in an uncontested space, rather than fighting for the same ones as your competitors. Blue ocean strategy is reconstructionist; it redefines former market boundaries, beliefs and industry structures. You don't aim to beat the competition, but rather avoid it.

The catch is, if you want to avoid competing, you must avoid the existing customers in your industry. If they are customers, they must be purchasing from one of your competitors and so you must compete to win their business. You must target non-customers instead.

Non-customers

There are three different types of non-customers.

1. Some are not customers yet, but they will eventually become customers, or they are marginal customers who purchase only when there are no alternatives. Pret A Manger, a fast-food chain, recognised that consumers with a preference for healthy food only had fast food when they were pressed for time. Pret developed an offering targeted at those non-customers and served them successfully. Typical fast-food customers do not find Pret particularly appealing, but Pret never wanted to compete with McDonald's or Burger King to begin with.

2. There are those who refuse to be customers because the typical value offered in your industry does not appeal to them. Gym bunnies and mothers do not buy advanced video game consoles, because they are not interested in that kind of entertainment. Nintendo famously launched its Wii console with non-customers in mind. It was

shunned by hardcore gamers because of its basic graphics and simple games, but families and children loved it precisely because of those features.

3. And there are non-customers who simply have never considered your industry. For example, fashion and cosmetic house Chanel introduced a line of make-up for men, a demographic that had never shown much interest in this industry before.

Serving non-customers requires numerous adjustments. Pret's food is unlike that of other fast-food restaurants, Nintendo's games were unlike those for Microsoft's or Sony's consoles, and men's make-up is unlike that for women. Deliberately targeting non-customers is the most common approach to blue ocean strategies, but some companies take a different approach.

Value innovation

It's easy to admire Starbucks, the global coffee chain, for how it intentionally created a coffee experience that stood in stark contrast to traditional coffee shops. Those shops catered only to customers looking for cheap, simple coffee quickly that they would consume outside on their way to somewhere else.

The CEO of Starbucks, Howard Schultz, who bought the original company (founded in 1971 when it was a coffee bean roaster and reseller), believed that the café experience he found in Italy would attract Americans to a different type of coffee shop. He remodelled Starbucks to allow customers to linger with their coffee in comfortable chairs, with Wi-Fi access and interior design that resembles a European café or a library more than a fast-food restaurant, creating a culture of sophistication and a perception of swank exclusivity. The company also expanded its menu to introduce flavours and variants that allow customers to personalise their order, grab some food, and conduct personal or business meetings at the same time. This new service did not attempt to compete on price with existing coffee shops. Nor did it attempt to offer a full menu that one might find at a fast-food or full-service restaurant.

Blue ocean strategy starts by considering an existing product or service in the market, perhaps offered by a competitor. It then suggests four different ways – often simultaneously – to innovate the value proposition of the existing product to create something new and useful.

1. **Elimination**. What value propositions might an innovator remove from an existing product? Starbucks eliminated table service. Unlike a traditional café, customers do not sit at a table with a menu. They do not wait for a member of the staff to give their order. And they do not simply sit quietly until their order is brought to their table.

2. **Reduction**. What features of an existing product might the innovator attenuate or push into the background? Starbucks reduced the value of affordability. In other words, it raised its prices. By itself, this action would most likely make customers less, not more, happy. It would reduce demand, not elevate it.

3. **Increase.** How might the innovator raise the emphasis of a feature that customers might enjoy, even if that increases the costs for the innovator? For example, Starbucks increased the comfort of its seating, encouraging patrons

to linger longer over their coffee. At first glance, this would not appear to be a winning strategy because each seat in the restaurant is filled for longer by a person who is purchasing only one cup of coffee, compared with traditional cafes that intentionally move people through the restaurant as fast as possible to make room for more customers.

4. **Creation**. What value propositions might unexpectedly thrill customers? Starbucks adds dark wood bookshelves, slate floors and soft music to make its coffee shop resemble a library more than a traditional cafe.

Kim and Mauborgne give the example of Cirque du Soleil, the entertainment company that travels from city to city and creates events under a big tent with a narrative arc, music and feats of daring from acrobats, much like a traditional circus. There are characters who function as clowns, others who have superhuman powers in gymnastics and trapeze, and others who pop up in the audience to surprise guests.

However, their performances are devoid of the one thing that traditionally signifies the circus: animals. There are no lions or elephants. Cirque du Soleil innovated on the centuries-old travelling circus. The Ringling Bros and Barnum & Bailey Circus eventually went out of business in 2017 after 146 years of ever-intensifying competition, with almost no innovation in its offering. Cirque du Soleil created a new market that had not previously existed by eliminating some features and adding others. It did not attempt to compete directly with traditional circuses. The customers of traditional circuses are parents, dragged by their children. But professionals and corporates were non-customers. Cirque du Soleil offered a refined circus entertainment to high-end customers. It even did so while spending *less* than traditional circuses – imagine how much money it saved by not having to support and transport dozens of exotic animals across North America or Europe. Cirque du Soleil did not improve the circus. It invented a new genre of entertainment.

Challenges of blue ocean strategy

The blue ocean strategy has garnered much acclaim, but some critics are not convinced that it represents a useful approach to innovation. Although the strategy adds some granularity to Christensen's advice to build products that create new markets, where should we find new features to create? In other words, the blue ocean strategy reinforced the need for innovators to think creatively, but how should we do that specifically? Where should we look?

*

There are many examples of companies that have attempted to innovate by eliminating seemingly favourable features of a product only to receive a tepid customer response. In other words, just because a product is novel does not make it useful. It's possible that a particular market segment is blue and uncontested because there are neither competitors nor potential customers. Ideas generated under the banner of the blue ocean strategy still require a process to verify that customers would find these innovators useful.

How to think creatively, refine new ideas and ensure their success are the subjects of the next chapter.

5

Refining innovation

When Galileo looked at the movement of stars in the sky, he concluded that the Earth was not the centre of the universe. "*Si muove*": it moves. The Earth, he concluded, revolves around the Sun. This was not a fact. It was a new *hypothesis* that Galileo knew would require – and merit – further testing. The word hypothesis has gained traction in the field of innovation as the core of a series of processes to describe, test and refine a new idea to ensure that, if and when the product or service is launched, customers will find that it solves a problem that they encounter in their lives.

The *Oxford English Dictionary* defines hypothesis as "a supposition or proposed explanation made on the basis of limited evidence as a starting point for further investigation". Smart organisations have been conducting this kind of testing and research around new products and innovations for decades. However, the function of market research has traditionally been dedicated to assessing sales opportunities in terms of market size, demographics and price points. Only recently have innovators been questioning key assumptions about the nature of the problems that customers seek to address or the optimal solutions for those problems.

Innovators initially met this notion of hypothesis testing

with scepticism. Innovation was viewed as the confluence of entrepreneurial verve and market opportunity. Process had no role in it. Researchers assumed that if it seemed like a good idea, it needed to get out into the marketplace as soon as possible because the first to arrive wins. Innovators were therefore encouraged to go to market quickly and make tweaks and adjustments after launch. Many start-ups did not build prototypes and did not collect feedback until the product was already in the market, with the downside that by then it was too expensive to fix any flaw.

Lean start-up method

The lean start-up method addresses this problem. One of its early founders is Steve Blank, a successful Silicon Valley entrepreneur with numerous start-ups to his name and a lecturer at both Stanford and Columbia universities. Noting how many start-ups never even speak to customers before spending years perfecting their product, Blank began telling entrepreneurs as early as the 1990s first to "get out of the building" to test their assumptions using actual consumer opinions before committing substantial time or resources to product development. He sought to instill a more scientific approach to early-stage entrepreneurial endeavour, using hypothesis testing among potential customers. He called this process "customer development".[1]

Blank's ideas were picked up and popularised by Eric Reis, an entrepreneur in Silicon Valley who coined the term "lean start-up," and saw it as an extension of the agile method for software development (see Chapter 2).[2] Reis's objective was to ensure that innovations were based on validated learning and experimentation. He believed that innovators must demonstrate empirically that their team "has discovered valuable truths about a start-up's present and future prospects" before the company gives the team more resources to move from ideation to implementation.

Reis especially advocated that innovators conduct "iterative product releases" with inexpensive, rapid, successive prototypes. The goal should be to create a minimum viable product (MVP), meaning a bare-bones prototype that potential customers would buy, even if they would prefer more features or design changes later. This experiment is more than just theoretical inquiry; it is a first product. If successful, it allows a manager to get started with his or her campaign: enlist early adopters, add employees to each further experiment or iteration, and eventually start to build a product. By the time that product is ready to be distributed widely, it will already have established customers. It will have solved real problems and offer detailed specifications for what more needs to be built.

Reis shifted the focus of innovators from "Can this product be built?" to "Should this product be built?" and then "Can we build a sustainable business around this set of products and services?"

Does the lean start-up method work?

Does the lean start-up methodology make a difference to eager innovators who believe they have an incredible idea that must get into the marketplace before anyone else creates it? We decided to investigate the question empirically using a pitch competition among teams of business students from hundreds of business schools around the world. The teams were seeking funding for their idea from a panel of judges, so there were real rewards to motivate the young entrepreneurs.

The competition focused on business model innovation, not technological innovation. After collecting data on the efforts of the winning teams, the study was able to draw concrete conclusions about the value of hypothesis testing. The entrepreneurial teams that employed the scientific method using hypothesis testing increased their likelihood of winning overall by 2.6 times compared with those teams that relied on gut instincts and flash of light epiphanies. For every hypothesis that a team in the sample confirmed, their chance of success in the competition increased by 3.3%. A team that confirmed ten hypotheses saw its chance of winning increase by 33%.

Even more interesting, every hypothesis that a team rejected, based on evidence from customers, generated an increase of 4.6% for their probability of success. Wait a minute. This conclusion finds that innovations that many customers do not find valuable are more likely to become more valuable in the long term. It's proof that, when innovators test and confirm a hypothesis about the potential impact of a new idea, they might indeed be solving a customer's problem. However, it is also possible that the innovator is collecting and interpreting the reactions from customers in a more positive way than those customers reflected. The innovator is succumbing to confirmation bias.

Innovators with a track record of rejecting lots of hypotheses, however, are demonstrating that they are objectively analysing and interpreting customer feedback, as we discussed in Chapter

1. The lean start-up method works because it introduces external evidence and encourages innovators to arrive at a more objective interpretation of that evidence.

The lean start-up method uses hypothesis to encourage and leverage objectivity. The trait empowers the process. The process works. Thus, the process reinforces the trait.

Constructing hypotheses

How should innovators create hypotheses? The first step is to make assumptions about the problems that customers face. These might derive from observation (the ethnography described in Chapter 4) or they might emerge from an innovator's experience or conversations with others.

The innovator might also make some assumptions about what solutions would solve the problem more efficiently and impactfully. These might emerge from analogies of disruptive innovation, result from exercises in design thinking or the blue ocean strategy. They might come from experts or customers outside the walls of your own company through open innovation.

Wherever the assumptions come from, the next step is to translate this assumption in a formal, testable, falsifiable hypothesis. The term "falsifiable" is important. If we state an assumption or hypothesis in such a way that we can never prove it is wrong, we have backed ourselves into a corner. For example, the assertion "This product will succeed" is not falsifiable. We can always define "succeed" in such a way that at least one customer using the product will not hurl it to the ground in disgust.

The goal of hypothesis testing is to attempt to prove,

actively and transparently, that your assumptions are wrong. Those assumptions that survive this critical scrutiny are worth further investment as the basis for an innovation.

There is a simple formula for constructing a powerful hypothesis. The generalised format is in the form of a conditional "if" statement, followed by a "then" clause stating a concrete result, such as: "If X then Y." If the entrepreneur has a specific idea or innovation in mind, the hypothesis is best phrased to express a positive supposition. For instance, compare these:

By using a smartwatch, a customer will be healthy.

vs

By using a smartwatch that tracks and reports steps taken per day, 50% of prototype customers will begin walking the recommended 8,000 steps per day for improved health within one month.

The first hypothesis is too broad: there is no concrete or specific definition of "healthy", and no duration over which this change should occur. It is also not falsifiable; it can never be proved wrong. The second hypothesis is much better. It clearly states a supposition that can be scientifically measured and proven correct. It also declared causality – that X causes Y, that the innovation in question can bring about the change desired. This type of hypothesis is both testable and falsifiable within a specific time frame that gives the innovator the ability to confirm or reject the hypothesis.

Pivots

When an innovator rejects a hypothesis, that is not the end of the game. The innovator must alter the assumption with a different idea, and then begin the testing process again. Adherents to the lean start-up method call this a pivot.

This is a magical word because it inserts optimism into what otherwise might seem like a failure. When an innovator rejects a hypothesis, it means that the innovator's initial assumption was wrong. The innovator failed to make an accurate guess about what customers want and need. The word "pivot" applauds the realisation, encourages the innovator to try again, and shows progress in the learning journey. A long series of pivots demonstrates that the innovator is getting closer and closer to a confirmed supposition that can be the basis for a valuable innovation.

There are many famous pivots in the history of innovation. The website Pinterest started as an e-commerce site for direct sales of products to consumers. Its initial tests concluded that this idea was not valuable to customers. It pivoted to become a visual social networking site, abandoning the notion of product sales. This new configuration has been wildly successful. YouTube, Google's video-sharing service, originally started as an online video dating site. The founders noticed that its visitors were less interested in finding a date and more interested in uploading short, personal and often funny videos.

A painful case study

Our research into the process of hypothesis testing is not just an academic investigation. Ted's own experience as an entrepreneur in Silicon Valley has been shaped by successes

– and failures – to use hypotheses. One example centred on a start-up that built an internet-connected smartwatch in 2011. The team had several of the top minds in marketing and engineering. It had ample funding and a partnership with one of the best manufacturers in the world for building consumer electronics. Almost everyone in Silicon Valley agreed that the market was ripe for a device that could bring alerts from a smartphone onto a person's wrist, and simultaneously collect data about a person's physical condition and send it to a smartphone. Despite these resources, the company could not sell its product.

In the process of designing the product, the team had made several assumptions about how customers and partners would value a product, but never tested these assumptions. Several of them proved to be wrong. For example, the product designers assumed that customers charged their smartphones every night, and therefore would be equally comfortable charging their smartwatch every night. In fact, it turned out that customers did not think about smartwatch charging technology alongside their smartphones. They compared the watches with a traditional analogue watch, which requires a new battery only once every few months.

The team could have learned about these nuances of customer and partner expectations if members of the company had constructed hypotheses and then had conversations to test them. The resulting pivots might have saved the company.

Eventually, the team ran out of money and patience. The company was sold to Google, where it became the foundation for the Wear OS software, which now runs smartwatches from Motorola, Fossil, Samsung, Michael Kors, Suunto and a dozen other brands. The sale may sound like a victory, but it was not the group's goal. The team had wanted to start and dominate the market for smartwatches. The launch of products using Google's software, along with the Apple Watch and a handful of other brands, testifies to the market opportunity. If the process for designing the innovation had been more rigorous, the players in the industry might be very different.

Other benefits of hypothesis testing

In addition to verifying demand, innovators enjoy three additional benefits of testing hypotheses.

1. The testing helps accumulate knowledge. A hypothesis that is not valid today might become valid in the future, because customer habits and tastes evolve. Keeping the data and conclusions about these tests acts like a repository of wisdom that entrepreneurs can dip into if they notice new market trends or develop new innovative ideas.

2. Even invalid hypotheses can point the way towards additional gaps in the market that might benefit from a completely different innovation. The evolution of Spotify over the course of the pandemic in 2020 exemplifies this. The company was relying heavily on advertising revenues that its millions of free users had to listen to in exchange for the music. When covid-19 hit and advertisers and agencies cut back, Spotify had to develop a new business model. Noticing the growth of podcasts as original content, Spotify began producing its own podcast content for its consumers, generating a new source of revenue.

3. The third benefit of hypothesis testing is championed by Rita McGrath at Columbia Business School. It revolves around the idea of optionality, where an innovative company might pursue a feature or business model that seems suboptimal in the moment, but that allows it to proceed in other directions that can prove valuable in the future.

Take, for example, a three-wheeled car like the Can-Am Spyder. This vehicle resembles a cross between a sub-compact traditional four-wheeled car and a beefy two-wheeled motorcycle. Demand for such a product is currently limited, so why produce it? The answer is that it allows the innovator an opportunity to learn a lot about engines, transmissions and suspensions that might have applications in the cars of the future. However, innovators should use this rationale sparingly and with caution, because it might easily become a false justification for confirmation bias.

Limits of the lean start-up method

Despite its power for designing impactful, profitable innovations, the lean start-up method also has a few flaws: sources, significance, stability and stopping. A story illustrates both the power of the lean start-up method and these hurdles. One of our MBA students, Alejandro, was leading a team to consider a new business focused on providing additional, curated information to visitors in national parks throughout the United States. We asked him to come up with several hypotheses about the attributes and expectations of the venture's most likely customers.

He responded that "consumers will enjoy what we build". By this statement, it was clear that Alejandro and his team did not understand where to start. In other scientific disciplines, researchers start their search for a good hypothesis by reading about what other researchers in the same field have already tested. This is the purpose of the literature review in a scientific paper. Hypotheses in those papers are often incrementally different from hypotheses that others have defined and explored.

Innovators have no such shoulders to stand on. They must craft new assumptions about customer demand without much prior reference. These assumptions are rarely incremental. They are more often large leaps away from what existing companies have already tested.

This is a problem of source. Where are the first hypotheses supposed to come from? The best route through this mystery is to consider analogies: what assumptions are vital for the success of existing products that our target customers also use? For example, if trying to determine good hypotheses for a new type of electric roller skates for commuters in large urban areas, an innovator might start with the key assumptions that support the launch of new basketball sneakers and commuter bicycles.

Eventually, Alejandro crafted some specific, falsifiable hypotheses. He also identified a likely target segment and started to conduct interviews. He returned to class to report that some people did indeed have the problems he assumed and would be eager to try the solution he envisioned. And other people did not. He asked: "How much verification is enough?" And our answer is: "Unfortunately, there is no standard."

This is also a problem that is not unique to innovation. In other scientific disciplines, researchers around the world have agreed on a threshold to declare that something is confirmed: there is less than a 5% chance that the hypothesis is wrong. That is the basis for declaring that something is "statistically significant" rather than non-significant. However, this universal threshold has no relevance for innovators.

If an innovator creates a new idea that will cost only a few dollars to test and launch, they might decide that hypothesis tests that show only a hint of confirmation might be enough. However, an innovator might conclude that an overwhelming majority of confirmation from a wide swath of hypotheses across a large sample of potential customers is not sufficient to warrant the launch of a product if it requires huge expense and risk. Such an innovator might continue to refine the idea and its hypotheses until customer response is unanimous.

After 50 interviews and several changes to the core idea, Alejandro and his team concluded that there was sufficient merit to develop a prototype. Their next question was: "When should we launch it?"

This seemingly simple question leads to a third intractable flaw in the lean start-up method. It does not tell an innovator how long the hypotheses remain confirmed. Customer demand changes, sometimes dramatically and quickly. Innovators cannot predict when a competitor or substitute product will enter the market to address some or all of the customers' latent problems. Or when an economy will crash, draining customer wallets and changing consumption patterns. In short, demand is not stable.

This stands in contrast to the most famous illustrations

of the scientific method. Newton found the force of gravity that applies to all contexts (at least until Einstein's theory of relativity). When Darwin discovered the process of evolution, he did not worry that the process had only existed for a week and would disappear a week later. This flaw does not mean that innovators should reduce their expectations for confirmation in order to move quickly. It does mean that innovators should track what other products or circumstances might change the value of the data they have already collected.

Towards the end of the course, Alejandro was sufficiently excited by his idea that he wanted to continue to pursue it even after graduation. His interviews showed a preponderance of evidence for a large, durable demand from customers who would enjoy – and pay for – a travel service. His final question to us was: "When should I stop testing and launch?" Again, this is a question that the lean start-up method does not know how to answer.

A traditional researcher's goal is to test and report. Failure to confirm a hypothesis may be the end of a research project. The game is different for an innovator attempting to use the scientific method. Just as there is no clear threshold for when to declare that a hypothesis has enough supporting evidence to be confirmed, there is no clear threshold for when an innovator has accumulated enough confirmed hypotheses to launch or enough rejected hypotheses to quit.

When to launch

One path out of this trap is evolve the nature of the hypotheses to embrace revenues and costs. Alejandro's hypothesis initially focused on customer problems and qualitative assessments of customer demand for his solution. As these are confirmed, he could move to a hypothesis that says: "Twenty out of the 100 people I approach will agree to pay $5 per month for the service and will continue the service for at least two months." He might also hypothesise: "After parsing the product into ten different features, I assert that I can construct and launch a product with only one feature, using no more than 10% of my budget, in order to generate the demand and revenue noted in the preceding hypothesis." These two hypotheses capture revenue and cost to arrive at a specific expectation for profitability. This process might be better labelled the lean management method as the innovator moves from design to launch to scale to profitability.

Another common path for innovators to escape the potentially endless loop of hypothesising and testing relies on time. Herb Simon, winner of a Nobel Prize for economics, coined the term "satisficing" to note that most managers cannot wait for the perfect solution and must suffice with one that is merely satisfactory. Running out of precious resources – investment, energy, passion and especially time – can push an innovator off the rigorous search for evidence into a more definitive go/no go decision.

A final path to stop the lean start-up method relies on instinct. Once a person's brain has determined that new information fits into existing models in the brain (see Chapter 1), an innovator's confidence in the product and in their own ability to launch the product disappears. This decision lies at the confluence of evidence, judgement and "gut feel".

The lean start-up method for you

Very few innovations emerge fully formed from an epiphany. Instead, innovations emerge from a disciplined process that tests the assumptions underlying a new idea and refines it through pivoting. Innovators need to carry out an objective assessment of an innovation, using evidence from potential customers, before committing significant resources to develop, build and deliver a product.

Using hypothesis testing and the lean start-up method has three key advantages. The first is that the process increases the likelihood of creating an impactful product. The second is that the process reduces the likelihood of wasted time, money, energy and reputation.

The third returns to the subjects we discussed in Part 1. By using hypotheses, individuals – even those who do not think that they are creative or confident or objective – can begin to develop an innovator's mindset. The process drives those behaviours. Once a person has successfully practised them, they develop self-efficacy for innovation, which in turn blossoms into entrepreneurial orientation.

Similarly, organisations that embrace, practise and reward the use of hypotheses across three horizons – near-, mid- and long-term – are more likely to practise ambidexterity, with projects that continue to exploit existing opportunities with existing products while simultaneously creating new innovations for new markets. Because hypothesis testing during ideation is faster and more efficient than developing, building and launching products that fail to address important customer problems, the consistent, repeated use of hypothesis testing inside an organisation makes it more agile, propelling it to sense and seize opportunities more effectively. In other words, the lean start-up method both leverages and creates the innovative attributes of organisations.

PART 3

Themes and trajectories in innovation

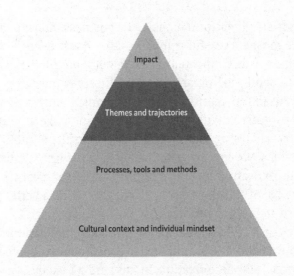

Impact

Themes and trajectories

Processes, tools and methods

Cultural context and individual mindset

After discussing the mindset and context for successful innovators, and introducing the state-of-the-art toolkit for innovation, in Part 3 we review many proven solutions to innovation problems. These recurring patterns and themes emerge and consolidate because they are especially effective. For example, 90% of all business model innovations are a recombination of existing business model patterns, like the choice of which customers to serve, how to sell to them, and what revenue models and cost structures work best. The old patterns of the company–customer relationship have undergone significant change, as business model innovation introduces new logic in how to create value for customers and how to capture some of this value for the organisation.

Chapter 6 looks at how companies have been finding innovative ways to charge a fee for their products and services to generate revenue. In Chapter 7 we detail the rise and growth of multi-sided platform models, the business model of choice for the most successful companies of the 21st century, where customers are connected directly with product or service vendors while the organisation itself serves only to provide the transaction platform. Another consolidating theme is innovation in a digital space, by leveraging large amounts of data and analysing them with advanced artificial intelligence techniques. We cover this in Chapter 8. In the final chapter, we look at innovation for social impact, aiming at creating value for a range of stakeholders by making the world a better place, but also at doing so profitably.

Each of these is a trajectory by which an innovation can be introduced and/or disseminated to consumers or adapted to fit new models of value creation. In this part, we encourage you to seek inspiration to rethink how you can deploy innovation for maximum impact.

6

Innovative pricing

The coffee business is not what it used to be. Think, for example, of how Nespresso has altered the traditional coffee world. In the old model, coffee was sold as a commodity in high quantities at low margins almost exclusively in retail stores. The companies that sold coffee did not also make the machines that roasted, ground, brewed and heated the coffee. Then along came Nespresso. It sold direct to consumers specially designed coffee machines to accommodate innovative single-use coffee cups (K-cups) at a high profit margin, targeted at offices and high-end households. In the past decade, many new coffee companies have launched using other innovative revenue ideas, such as a subscription business model, a socially conscious fair trade business model, a "freemium" giveaway model, and a bricks-and-clicks retail/online sales model.

How companies choose which audience to target, how to attract and market to those consumers, and what price points and profits they need are all elements of a company's business model. The right model will generate the revenues a company needs to sustain itself and grow. The old patterns of manufacturer – middleman distributor and retailer, each with their respective customary profit margin – are being replaced by a host of new business models. Companies today may even experiment with their revenue models, shifting from one approach to another to test the markets and discover their best option(s).

In this chapter, we will explore eight highly valued revenue models that companies are adopting to innovate their business models, ranging from freemium to the razor-and-blade model and from auction to the subscription.[1] All have roots in traditional revenue models but with new twists and mutations largely based on the use of technology across all aspects of the business.

Customer segmentation with "freemium"

Since the 15th century, chefs have made gelatin, a clear jelly-like product produced from boiled bones, hooves and connective tissues of animals. Gelatins were often used to make desserts look shiny and add to their flavour – a finesse largely for the wealthy until 1845, when industrialist Peter Cooper patented a technique to make powdered gelatin, which made it easier to use and cook. But the real success of gelatin in dessert making occurred in 1897 when husband and wife team Pearle Bixby and May Wait mixed fruit flavours and sugar with powdered gelatin and sold the formula in 1899 to the Genesee Pure Food Company, which branded it with the name Jell-O.

The product sold only moderately for a few years until Genesee's owner, Francis Woodward, had a brilliant stroke of innovative genius. He wrote and printed a cookbook featuring Jell-O recipes and used an army of salespeople to hand out free copies of it. Consumers loved the free book and sales of Jell-O rocketed.

This idea of giving away something for free to drive sales

was unheard of in that era. But since then, it has grown to be among the most common strategies in marketing. In the 1950s, banks often gave away a free toaster for opening a new savings account. In the 1970s, an entire industry of free promotional merchandise exploded with giveaways of all kinds, from wearable items to calculators to car accessories, especially printed with a company's logo or a product's brand name. It soon became a no-brainer in marketing to recognise that consumers love giveaways and will often decide to purchase a product if something free is added into the deal.

In the early years of digital technology, the strategy of giving consumers something at no cost to appeal to their sense of receiving a bargain helped launch a new type of get-something-for-free – the "freemium model". The term represents something of a mixed model: consumers receive a baseline of something for free followed by additional "premium" layers of service or benefits that must be paid for. The freemium model was especially effective for selling products with embedded communication technology because use limits can be programmed into software until extra functionality is bought by consumers.

Among the first freemium-type deals was the software designed to run on the PalmPilot personal digital assistant (PDA). To increase the value of each PalmPilot handheld computer, Palm Inc. encouraged buyers to download apps for their device. Many of these apps were free, but some would provide only limited functionality or operate only for a limited period, enticing satisfied users to pay for a fully functional version. The freemium model was so successful that many members of the Palm team that developed the software eventually migrated to Apple to launch its now-legendary App Store.

Today, examples abound of how digital hardware and software companies use the freemium model to attract users for free, hook them into loving a product, and then upsell them for higher-level services. For example, the multi-player online game *Fortnite* boasts 250 million players and most aspects of the game do not require any payment whatsoever. Once players have learned the rules, completed some adventures and earned a sense of accomplishment, they can voluntarily make small payments to improve their experience and accelerate their victories. These micro-payments add up quickly. Epic Games, the owner of *Fortnite*, generates revenues of billions of dollars each year through these in-game micro-payments.

One way to explain the success of free products is with the micro-economic notion of price elasticity. Technically, elasticity is defined as the impact on demand for each change in price. An inelastic item (such as a glass of lemonade in the middle of a long, hot hike; a unique drug to fight cancer; or the price of electricity to power lights in a home) shows almost no change in quantity demanded even when the price changes. An elastic item – like the price of a sports or concert ticket – shows huge changes in quantity demanded even for small changes in price.

The freemium model offers free products to those people for whom the product is highly elastic. This strategy encourages them to use the product and, once they use it, find that it solves a problem in a novel way. Often, this realisation means that the customer will not abandon the product if the price rises. Their elasticity changes from elastic towards inelastic, and the innovator can raise the price above $0.

The takeaway is this: do not offer free products to people who are not price-sensitive. If they are willing to pay a high price, there is not much benefit to lowering the price; the quantity that they desire will not change.

The freemium model has numerous advantages in attracting consumers to a product or service, but there are also drawbacks to consider. Chief among these is an overreliance on the free element to attract customers and keep them. Dubbed the "Zero to One problem" by Peter Thiel, a prominent venture capitalist in Silicon Valley and co-founder of PayPal, he notes that too many entrepreneurs rely on "free" for customer growth.[2] When it comes time to raise the price above $0, many of these customers disappear. In his view, the free offer fails to factor in what often become poor conversion rates, with new customers failing to convert to paying ones. Free might attract users, but it does not necessary generate revenue and it can become a recipe for large losses.

There's also the danger that, in a company that offers a wide range of products or services, those that include a freemium model can devalue the firm's other products and even all similar products from other vendors. An example is how free "headline" news sites on the internet have detracted from many subscription-model news sites. Very few people will now pay for a full subscription to media outlets because they are used to reading just the headlines for free. This is known as a "race to the bottom" for many innovators.

A third drawback is that when a product is free, customers might intentionally consume only that portion of it. This is the equivalent of putting free mint candies in a bowl at your reception desk. There are customers who will come into the office just to grab handfuls of them and never bother becoming clients. Innovators need to keep this type of potential customer in mind and aim to keep them in "economics" mode, recognising that there is a tacit business transaction involved. For example, Groupon entices businesses to provide large discounts so that it can help them attract more customers. In the restaurant industry, many Groupon clients have suffered from an abundance of customers who purchase the discounted deals and never spend more on a meal than Groupon allocates and only return if another Groupon discount is offered. The restaurant thus fails to develop new loyal customers who will eat there even without a Groupon offer.

Despite these challenges, a price of $0 can be an innovation: it solves a customer's problem in a novel and impactful way. Until this point in the book, we have assumed that an innovation is a new product or service. This creative of use of pricing marks an interesting shift in this assumption. An innovative company can offer a product that already exists in a market for a price, but instead offer it for free with an alternative way to generate revenue. The innovation is not the product; it is the way that the innovator charges a fee (or not) for the product.

Free services with hidden revenues

Another revenue approach leverages the attractiveness of a free offering. It also does so by abandoning the received wisdom that revenue should come from customers or users. Instead, the revenue is concealed deeper in the business model while users can enjoy free services.

The email account you don't pay for is one example. The numerous social media platforms you enjoy free of charge are another. So are the free newspapers and magazines you can read on public transport and even the benches you sit on in a park or while waiting for a bus. But none of these are truly free. They are costly to make and somebody has to pay for them. It's just not the customer. This type of revenue model rests on an innovative separation between revenue and customer, with the revenue hidden from the customer.

Let's look into the most successful application of this model in greater detail. The most popular search engine, as well as its company's top product, Google Search has always been free for its users. Businesses pay for it through advertisements. One of the main value propositions of this type of digital advertising is that it can target specific users or categories of users, and so generate more sales.

In the age of billboards and TV ads, the same customers were exposed to ads promoting cleaning products, cars, insurance, confectionery, sanitary products, cosmetics and more. Most viewers of these ads were simply the wrong target. So any money spent on targeting them was wasted. John Wanamaker, the founder of the eponymous department stores, complained: "Half the money I spend on advertising is wasted. The trouble is I don't know which half." Advanced data analytics helps Google to optimise the targeting of ads and so helps businesses to grow revenues. Indeed, hidden revenues are typically supported by businesses through advertising.

In Google's platform model (see Chapter 7), publishers also play an important role. They create new content that attracts readers and then allow advertisements to appear on their sites, for which they receive a payment. Variants of this model fill the coffers of social media giants and other digital behemoths.

The hidden exchange consists in a valuable free service for the users in return for the authorisation to harvest users' data. These companies leverage such data (see Chapter 8) to optimise advertising services that are then sold to businesses. Although many users happily accept this exchange, abuse on the part of these companies has led to the concern that, if it's free to you, you must be the product.

This ads-based hidden revenue model is not exclusive to digital companies. Advertising company JCDecaux installs a range of urban physical infrastructures and street furniture, like garbage bins, benches, bus stops and public bicycle rental systems. It does so free of charge to the city or the transport network, and of course to the citizens using them. In return, it manages advertising spaces on all these street furniture and billboards. Once again, it is advertising that generates revenues to pay for products and services that are free to customers and users.

Customer lock-in with razor-and-blade pricing

When Standard Oil entered the Chinese market at the end of the 19th century, it created great demand for its kerosene by giving away 8 million lamps for free or at very cheap prices. Indeed, when households had acquired a lamp, they started buying more and more kerosene. The same business logic lay behind King Camp Gillette's recognition that, if he sold the razor handle and a few disposable blades at a low price, customers would buy more razor blades from the Gillette company for years thereafter. The overall revenue from each customer would be higher than if he had sold them a single product only once. Since then, many companies that manufacture both a durable item and accompanying consumables have used this model.

For example, Hewlett-Packard sells most of its printers at low price to consumers with a low profit margin. It then sells ink refills for those printers at high prices with high margins. The former behemoth of film photography, Eastman Kodak, sold its cameras at a low cost and so enjoyed high margins on its films. The Nespresso coffee machines follow the same pattern of low-cost hardware with a high-cost consumable that must be used with that hardware. Consumers who buy Apple hardware, such as iPhones and iPads, are locked into purchasing their music and other content from the iTunes store.

Economists define the term "lock-in" as the status of a customer who has decided to stick with the same product even if its price rises. Lock-in is a psychological decision that a customer makes, involving both logic and emotion. Companies can influence this decision in many ways. For example, developing a brand reputation for exclusivity can contribute to lock-in: many people purchase luxury goods from Louis Vuitton and Ferrari because they enjoy being identified as someone who can afford such obviously expensive products.

Lock-in is also a logical decision. Once a person has purchased an HP printer and it runs out of ink, they have two options: to purchase a new printer or to purchase new ink. If the price for new ink is slightly below the price of a new printer, the customer logically should purchase the new ink, even if the price of the ink is wildly higher than the cost that HP expended to manufacture and deliver the ink.

There are several problems with this model, however.

1. Consumers are becoming more savvy and resistant to being locked in. They might resent it, even if being locked

into a product gives them an increase in value. Being locked in becomes an obvious disincentive.

2. This kind of lock-in depends on the customer being unable to use other, cheaper razor blades or ink cartridges. Clever independent entrepreneurs have found ways around this by manufacturing similar products that can be used with the durable item. For instance, ink cartridge companies began selling compatible ink cartridges that worked in proprietary printers, forcing the printer manufacturers to upgrade their hardware so that it can recognise third-party cartridges. Other ink companies launched businesses that simply refilled the original cartridges, thus fooling the printers into detecting original cartridges. As a result, the model became a cat-and-mouse game between companies that produced the durable item and its consumables versus entrepreneurs who found ways to sell the consumables to consumers at cheaper prices.

3. The patent on the durable item can expire, opening the door to imitators who can jump in with cheaper versions of the durable item and the consumables. This occurred to Keurig which lost its patent on K-cup coffee pods in 2012, after which dozens of coffee companies (including Nespresso) jumped in with new models of coffee machines using K-cup inspired design and coffee brewing technology.

4. However tightly a company can arrange to lock in customers, it has the same flaw as any product: the possibility that another company creates a low-end disruptive innovation that eventually gains traction and takes over the market from the dominant player. The

original razor blade giant, Gillette, experienced this when numerous rivals began manufacturing a single, unified, disposable razor and handle of high quality at a low price. Customers could solve the problem of shaving without having to contemplate multiple pieces of a single product. Gillette has been forced to respond by lowering its price for blades and by making its own stand-alone disposable razors.

Recurring revenues through subscriptions

In the 1950s, millions of homes subscribed to a daily milk delivery service and both morning and evening newspapers. The paperboy appeared at weekends to collect the fees and a tip, and the milkman would drop by to collect cash or a cheque. Subscription was an excellent revenue model used by magazines, landscape and maintenance services, fuel companies and more.

As the population climbed, however, it became harder to collect subscriptions, until technology stepped in to change the equation. With online banking, and companies like PayPal, WePay and others that have made it easy for companies to set up recurring payments from their customers, the subscription model has expanded rapidly again and is now being used in a wide range of industries. The model has also been aided by inexpensive delivery and mail services from FedEx, UPS and DHL.

Several industries rely on subscriptions. Blue Apron in the United States and Mindful Chef in the UK sell fresh food that has already been portioned, sliced and packaged so that the ingredients are ready to cook in order to make a quick "homemade" meal. The company relies on subscriptions, where consumers pay a fee to a certain number of pre-measured boxed dinners per week. Consumers can choose from among many meal choices and each box is refrigerator packed and mailed. Dozens of companies have entered this market with variations on meal delivery by subscription.

Peloton entered the crowded fitness industry with an innovative idea: a monthly subscription that included its high-quality indoor training bicycle and access to video-based trainers. Neither Peloton's bicycle nor its training videos are dramatically different than those of hundreds of other suppliers. Its innovation was the subscription that gave access to both.

The subscription model offers many advantages for companies. First and foremost, it allows them to have greater predictability of their revenues because they can use accurate counts of subscribers and fees. Even if the number of subscribers varies each period, with people dropping out while others sign on, the patterns of losses versus gains can become predictable. A stable recurring revenue also allows the company to make better strategic decisions about its growth opportunities.

The subscription model can often make a product or service affordable for a demographic that may not be able to purchase a high-cost item, such as a car or even an expensive piece of home gym equipment. And having loyal subscribers who purchase every month gives the company unique opportunities to collect data and develop insights into its customers' buying habits and patterns. These insights can help the organisation develop better models for how to retain customers as well as how to attract new customers.

As with every revenue model, however, companies can encounter problems using the subscription model. Clever organisations will calculate in advance the churn rate per period – the number of subscribers lost versus gained – but their estimates may be far too low, causing them substantial revenue losses. What can be worse, however, is the cost of chasing and acquiring new customers, especially if the churn rate is high. Often referred to as the "customer treadmill", companies can spend far more than they planned due to higher-than-expected customer attrition.

The entertainment subscription company MoviePass went defunct in 2020 after less than a decade in business because of a potential flaw in its subscription model. The company promised subscribers a range of plans, from one film a day to three films a month to unlimited films. However, many cinema chains refused to join the MoviePass list of suppliers, largely because the subscription model would have undercut their own pricing and revenue.

Even with these challenges, the subscription model is a successful innovation for many new industries, with room to grow. For example, just as home insurance companies use a subscription model, we should expect to see home repairs companies, including plumbers, electricians and roofers, consider a subscription model to provide continuous service.

The subscription model has been a fixture for a long time in the clothing industry, providing fresh uniforms every day for cooks and janitors. This has expanded into up-market fashion: companies like Rent the Runway in the United States and Hurr in the UK allow subscribers to select and use a spectacular expensive designer dress for a fancy gala, and then return it the next day instead of having the garment sit idly in a wardrobe.

Delayed revenues: the hockey stick

The various innovations in generating revenue all presume that profitability is urgent. Many innovators do not face this constraint. They can afford to delay any attempt to charge a fee for their product, opting instead to grow awareness, quality or usage.

For example, Jeff Bezos, in his annual letter to investors and shareholders, repeated year after year that his goal was to spend heavily on promotion to customers, promotion to suppliers, features in the store like a recommendation engine, and ancillary product lines. Once the company dominated the blossoming category of online retail, it could contemplate profitability with fewer competitive pressures. Innovators expecting to raise money through advertising must assemble a large audience before advertising revenue becomes material.

In some circles, this approach is called the hockey stick projection: profits dip early, even creating a net loss for the company, until they reach an inflection point where the company has enough customer attention to attract revenue. The prediction concludes with a steep rise in profitability, earning the company a high valuation and sterling reputation (see Figure 3). This is the promise that almost all entrepreneurs present to early investors based on glowing but perhaps naive financial models. Not surprisingly, entrepreneurs employing this prediction are usually at the lowest point of the stick where revenues are small and costs are high, supporting the argument that the entrepreneur requires just a little more funding to reach the inflection point.

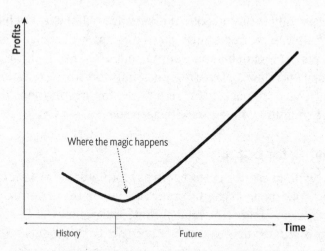

Figure 3. Hockey stick growth projections

More sophisticated investors are willing to believe in this glowing projection when innovators can objectively demonstrate large, untapped customer demand. Some venture capitalists are adopting the language and metrics of the lean start-up method, asking for the evidence that was accumulated during customer discovery to confirm hypotheses with minimum viable products. Innovations around pricing merit the same scrutiny as other types of product features: thorough testing before large-scale launch.

Google founders Sergey Brin and Larry Page started working on their search engine in their mythical garage in 1995. Three years later, the company was incorporated. Only three years after that, in 2001, the company was profitable for the first time. This was possible thanks to the investors' willingness to cover losses and investments for a long time.

One of the greatest threats to pursuing this strategy

successfully is running out of money. Indeed, the research on start-up post mortems by consulting company CB Insights (see Chapter 4) highlights that running out of money is the main reason for failure. Delayed revenues only work for organisations that have deep pockets or, better still, for organisations that have committed investors with deep pockets.

Paying for outcomes

The willingness of a customer to pay for a product or a service does not depend primarily on its cost but on the performance it makes possible or the valuable outcome it allows. In Chapter 4 we discussed how a customer does not buy a product for its own sake, but for the job (functional, emotional or social) it helps get done. The principle of charging customers for the job done, or part thereof, can be called "paying for outcomes".

Performance-based contracts illustrate this. For example, aerospace manufacturer Rolls-Royce does not sell its aircraft engines. Instead, it charges by the hour for use, with a "power-by-the-hour" revenue model. Rolls-Royce retains ownership of the engine, along with the maintenance duties, and charges only for the time when the engine is used – and so creates value for the customer.

Similarly, printing devices maker Xerox has introduced a successful "managed print" set of services. For each of its clients, Xerox identifies the best printers and devices, including those made by other companies, and offers a service that includes maintenance, toner substitution, paper replenishment and periodical upgrades. All this is important, but the client does not appreciate its value. The client only cares about being able to print when it needs to. Accordingly, Xerox charges its clients for pages printed, often at a lower cost than traditional pricing models.

The unique approach of this model consists in transforming what used to be a product into a service. The provider retains ownership of its products. This changes many of the economic incentives of the traditional model. If your revenues depend on selling another printer, you will have every reason to make printers that need to be replaced every so often, so that you can sell a new one. If your revenues depend on the output each printer is capable of, regardless of how old it is, you will have an incentive to keep it running efficiently for a long time. This also encourages more sustainable business models that extend the life of products.

A champion of sustainability in industrial and commercial carpets – traditionally not a very environmentally friendly industry – follows precisely this approach. The US modular flooring company Interface does not sell carpets; it charges for carpet services. To do so more profitably and sustainably, it uses carpet tiles so that when parts of the carpets wear out, only the worn tiles need to be replaced instead of the entire floor. Moreover, it took inspiration from nature, with an approach called biomimicry, where forest floors are all different, because each square metre has a unique arrangement of grass and leaves and flowers. Interface now designs tiles with coloured patterns that can easily be mixed and matched to hide any discrepancy between old and new carpet tiles.

This pricing model is also widely applied in the digital space. Businesses don't just want customers to watch their advertisements. They want them to click on the banners that link to their websites. Hence one of the services of Google is called pay-per-click. As the name suggests, advertisers pay only when a viewer clicks on the ad, resulting in a visit to the advertiser's website.

Let the customers pay what they want

With an unconventional twist on the notion that companies should set the price for their products, some let their customers decide how much they want to pay. Sometimes the buyer can even pay nothing for a product, but more frequently minimum or suggested price brackets are given as guidance. The benefit of this model is that it makes products accessible to a much larger market, where each customer pays what they are willing to, and so cannot be priced out. This is especially effective for zero marginal cost goods, that is, goods for which extra units can be sold at no additional cost to produce.

UK rock band Radiohead made the 2007 album *In Rainbows* available to download through its website. For the three months before the official release date, fans could pay whatever they wanted for the digital version of the album. The band earned more money with this than with any of its six previous albums. Surprisingly, sales of *In Rainbows* were unaffected after the record reached the stores. This experiment worked particularly well for two reasons. On the one hand, once the songs are written and recorded, extra digital copies carry no additional cost. On the other hand, Radiohead fans happily paid for their physical copy of the record even though they had a chance to get it for free.

It is not only loyalty at play here. General moral norms encourage customers to pay for valuable goods. In 2013, e-commerce headset.com offered its customers the option to pay what they wanted. The CEO later reported that only 10% chose to pay less than full price.

A deliberate moral motive can rest behind pay-what-you-want. The US bakery Panera Bread opened a pay-what-you-want café in 2010, catering to customers who cannot afford to pay for a good meal. The logic was that more affluent customers would pay more and so subsidise meals for the customers who chose to pay less. Regrettably this model failed in the long run, but not because of its pricing model. Rather, affluent customers did not want to have their meals sitting next to homeless people. And people who were food insecure felt that eating there attached a stigma to their condition, as the company was offering just one discounted meal per week or to do volunteer work at the restaurant in exchange for a free meal.

This may not have been the right pricing model in the restaurant industry, where marginal costs remain fairly constant even when more meals are prepared. Research shows that – unsurprisingly – the pay-what-you-want model results in higher sales but lower earnings per customer.

There are occasions where this is exactly what a company wants. For example, some theatres and zoos allow spectators and visitors to pay what they want on empty seats for certain shows or for last-minute availability.

Clothing retailer Everlane has found another interesting way to leverage this pricing model. For its discounted products during seasonal sales, it lets customers choose one of three prices. The lowest suggested price is sufficient to cover Everlane's costs to produce and ship the product; the middle price also covers overhead for their staff, and the highest price covers costs and adds a modest profit to be reinvested in the business. Customers like this transparency and think of seasonal sales differently, in a way that preserves the perception of value.

Auctioning to the highest bidder

Another interesting spin on the notion that the seller determines the price for its goods is the auction. Historical reports by Herodotus describe the use of auctions as far back as 500BC but auctions are still in vogue and find innovative applications in the 21st century.

The principle of auctions is that the price is determined by the buyer who is willing to pay the highest price, usually within a given time frame. The probability of attracting a high price for a given item, therefore, depends on access to many prospective buyers. The internet has greatly expanded such access.

In the digital world, eBay was the pioneer of the online auction. Sellers listed their products at a low starting price and collected the price offered by the highest bidder. Additional conditions may complicate this model, like the reserve price to ensure a guaranteed minimum, or the second price where the highest bidder pays the price offered by the second highest bidder to mitigate winner's regret. At any rate, the key advantage for sellers is that they receive the highest acceptable price. Customers benefit in that they can influence the price of the item they intend to buy.

Auctions work best when many prospective buyers desire the same, scarce goods. For example, many airline passengers would be happy to fly on a higher class of service than their ticket, provided it costs less than buying a high-class ticket in the first place. Therefore, several airlines offer passengers the chance to upgrade by auctioning any unsold seats in business and first class ahead of each flight.

In digital marketing, many companies would like their brand to appear when a user runs a search. For example, we would love this book to appear on top of every Google search for "innovation". We are not the only ones. So to get the coveted spot we compete with others. Indeed, Google runs an ultra-rapid, automated auction for every search query. The highest bid has the highest chances of featuring in the search results.

The pricing is right

Innovations in pricing continue to emerge and evolve, with recombinations and extensions of the pricing patterns described above. For example, Dollar Shave Club combines multiple methods discussed in this chapter – freemium, subscription, aiming for lock-in – by giving away its proprietary razor for free to consumers who subscribe to its monthly razor blade delivery service. Google accepted delayed revenues, it generates hidden revenues and, for some of its ads, it charges performance-based prices, which are set through an auction mechanism.

All the same attitudes and techniques from our earlier chapters still apply to this kind of innovation. They still benefit from ethnography and design thinking. They may still disrupt existing products and companies with a new approach to affordability that brings new customers into the market. Innovators contemplating a price of $0 should still declare and test their hypotheses to confirm that customers will react to this price in the way that the innovator expects. Panera Bread would have been well advised to do so before finding that the customer experience it had designed for both the affluent and the less affluent did not appeal to either.

7

Multi-sided platforms

The earliest known example of a marketplace was the Greek agora in Athens. Started as a meeting place where people could gather to trade ideas, it evolved into a location where independent buyers and sellers convened to trade products. The utility of an open market made it a common fixture in Western European culture, and so it was only natural that it would be adopted into the digital age through "platform" businesses on the internet. Most of the most valuable companies in the world offer a multi-sided marketplace a core piece of their business: Alibaba, Alphabet (which owns Google), Amazon, Apple, Meta (which owns Facebook), Microsoft and Tencent.

The traditional method for companies to create value was to manufacture and deliver a product through wholesalers, middlemen and retailers until it reached the end-consumers. Platforms do not provide any of these features. Instead, the role of the company hosting the platform is to put consumers directly in touch with the vendors of the products or services, where the buyers and sellers are on different sides of the transaction (hence the "multi" in "multi-sided").

The goal of the platform host is to facilitate the connection between the sellers and the buyers for a mutually beneficial exchange. The platform host's value is derived from its function as a coordinator.

Multi-sided platforms have become ubiquitous across many industries and have dominated most of the industries they enter, stealing market share and profits from existing companies and relegating branded manufacturers to secondary status as just one vendor or supplier among many on a platform. Customers often lose their relationship to manufacturers or brands, migrating their attention and loyalty to the platform itself. For example, Amazon enjoys much more brand exposure and commitment than most of the brands that sell products on its platform.

The platform is an innovation in the way that companies can solve customer problems and deliver value. What seems like an ancient simple idea in fact rests on complexity and nuance. This chapter describes the key elements of a successful multi-sided platform to help innovators apply this business theme to other industries and locales. In other words, if you are not currently operating a platform business, you should. Otherwise, this type of business might well threaten the future of your own business.

The sharing economy

As the internet connected people, consumers started to realise that they had household items sitting idle that someone else might want to use. The dress in the wardrobe, the car in the garage, the sofa in the living room: the owner of the asset only needs them a few times a day at most. What if other people wanted them when the owner does not? Would this solve a problem for the recipient and generate some income for the owner? The key to the sharing economy lies in the ability for owners to loan these idle products and assets to someone else.[1] (An asset is just a broader term for any property that you control, including physical products, real estate, ideas and even your own time and energy.)

People with assets to share become sellers. People who want to use those assets become buyers. Note that, in the sharing economy, sellers do not fully sell the asset; they only rent its use. Buyers do not buy the asset; they purchase temporary access to its use for a fixed period. Because the recipient can solve a problem, typically at a lower price, by using a shared item, many transactions within the sharing economy expect and require payment, typically as a commission to the platform owner on top of the price that the buyer is giving the seller.

Uber, the ride-hailing service, is the epitome of the sharing economy. It allows people with idle cars to connect with people who prefer to use a car rather than a taxi or other form of public transport to go from one place to another. Uber is now one of the largest providers of point-to-point ground transport in the world, even though the company does not own a single car or employ a single driver. Its commissions on each journey continue to grow exponentially.

As you walk around your home and office, you can start to notice what expensive assets are under-used? Space, time, people, expertise – all these tangible and intangible resources have spare capacity that another person might value.

Designing a multi-sided platform

In 2010, the practice and research into entrepreneurship took a great leap forward with the introduction of the business model canvas by Alexander Osterwalder and Yves Pigneur.[2] This diagram changed how entrepreneurs think about designing a new venture in two different ways.

First, the canvas defines nine elements of a business model to help entrepreneurs develop a shared vocabulary and a common set of categories to organise hypotheses for testing and refine their business models: key partners, key activities, value propositions, customer relationships, customer segments, key resources, channels, cost structure and revenue streams. The canvas puts all these elements into a single diagram on one page, so that it's easy to see how the pieces of their business models fit together.

However, the business model canvas was designed for a linear business model, in which a company manufactures a product or service and then sells it through a distribution system with retailers or direct to customers. Platform entrepreneurs, company leaders and business educators needed a different type of planning tool optimised for designing multi-sided platforms. Together with two of his students, Marcel Allweins and Markus Proesch at Hult International Business School, Ted envisioned and created a new platform canvas, along with a video to demonstrate its use (see Figure 4).[3]

The platform canvas helps innovators design impactful new platforms. It also assists leaders in companies with traditional, linear business models to envision if and how a platform could jeopardise their market share and profitability. As you contemplate a new platform idea, this diagram gives you the

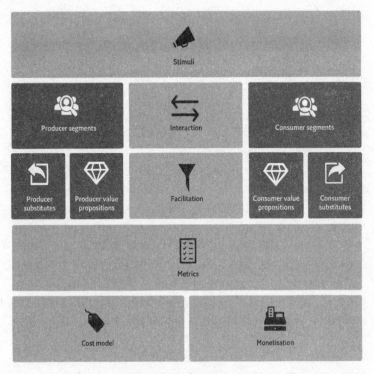

Figure 4. The platform canvas

recipe for constructing hypotheses that you can subsequently test.

The network effect

A fundamental principle in the success of a platform business is the network effect: that the value of each person on a platform is directly related to the number of other people on the platform. In effect, buyers need vendors who need more buyers who then need more vendors.

Uber is a prime example of the network effect. The first potential passenger on Uber's platform was not thrilled with the service. There were only a few drivers with cars available at any given time or place. But as more customers joined up, Uber attracted more drivers, which in turn increased the likelihood of finding an available Uber driver nearby. With more drivers available, people could count on getting a ride quickly, so more passengers then signed up.

The network effect is not an accident. It's a design choice that every innovator can make voluntarily that can be built into the way a company chooses to solve the customer's problem. Uber could have started its own taxi company by buying a fleet of new cars and employing thousands of drivers, with some clever web-connected smartphone apps for people to book a ride. Uber's innovation was in electing to build a multi-sided platform marketplace instead of a traditional transportation company. Point-to-point ground transport is not new. Taxi services are not new. What was new for this particular problem was a company that dedicated itself solely to connecting passengers with independent operators who already own a car. This innovation in the way that Uber structured its offering also changed the affordability of ground transport and its immediacy. Instead of walking to a taxi stand, people can expect a car to arrive at their door within a few minutes for a very low price.

Two network effects

There are two different types of network effect.

The **direct network effect,** in which more users of a particular service drives even more users. Amazon's ratings and reviews provide an illustration of this direct network effect. People who purchase a product can leave feedback that helps a subsequent customer make the decision to buy the product. The more people who buy the product on Amazon and leave a rating, the more valuable Amazon's marketplace becomes for each individual buyer. Crucially, Amazon does not employ people to rate and review products in the marketplace. Amazon expanded its platform features so that external purchasers can provide this value for other buyers. This is also called the "same side" network effect.

The **indirect network effect**, in which two different groups are at opposite sides of the buyer/seller divide, creating a virtuous cycle of growth. At Airbnb, for example, when there are more renters looking for a room or home on Airbnb, it produces greater demand for temporary lodging in a specific location. This demand persuades more homeowners to join Airbnb to offer their apartments for rent. The more apartments and homes for rent, the more renters who become interested in using Airbnb. This is called "indirect" because the value for each renter is dependent on the number of homeowners offering their units for rent. It is also called a "cross-side" network effect.

Balancing supply and demand

Although the network effect is a recipe for rapid growth, it is not a foolproof mechanism. If you launch an innovative, impactful platform, the first challenge you will encounter is balance: how to ensure that the number of buyers and sellers are equal. If a platform has too many buyers and not enough sellers, a large portion of buyers will not find the service they seek. This has four consequences.

1. With fewer consummated transactions, this imbalance reduces commissions for the company.

2. With too many buyers chasing only a few suppliers, the price of the rare goods is likely to be high. Although this is great for the sellers, it is not ideal over the long term for convincing more buyers to join the platform. High prices rarely invoke disruptive innovation.

3. This imbalance might resolve itself in the short term, where these unfulfilled buyers might leave the platform. However, it might have lasting impacts if the disappointed buyers elect never to return.

4. Any money that the company expended to recruit buyers was misspent and should have been deployed to recruit sellers instead.

Platform innovators have two primary levers to rebalance supply and demand: marketing and commissions. For example, a multi-sided platform called GetMyBoat runs a marketplace for boat owners to rent their boats for a few hours to people who want to enjoy an experience on the water. GetMyBoat's catalogue includes hundreds of different kinds of boats, from large yachts that come with a captain and crew, to small canoes and surf boards.

The typical buyers of the services at GetMyBoat are very different to the typical suppliers. Buyers are on vacation, with a few hours to spare for an adventure. They are willing to spend some money but usually have some financial limitations (if they were exceedingly rich, they would buy a boat themselves.) However, sellers are typically locals who live near water. They have an asset – the boat – that is sitting idle because they do not use it often. They are motivated either by the thought of a little extra cash or by the hope that visitors can enjoy the water without having to purchase a new product that they might use only once.

The two groups have different problems they wish to solve. GetMyBoat needs to reach them in different places on the internet. Buyers are googling "what to do in Kansas?" whereas sellers are googling "how to make some money from my used canoe".

GetMyBoat has two tracks in its marketing strategy, one for buyers and one for sellers. If the company finds that there are too many suppliers offering a wide variety of boats in hundreds of locations around the world but only a handful of buyers who are interested in renting those boats, it can decrease its budget for marketing to suppliers and increase its budget for marketing to buyers.

A platform can also rebalance supply and demand by changing its commission. Let's start with a simplified pricing system. The platform allows suppliers to post the price of their service. Buyers compare offers and select the one that has the most features at the lowest price. As a result, buyers and sellers find a rough market price for the service. That is the price that the buyer will pay to the platform. The platform then subtracts its commission and forwards the remainder to the seller.

A high commission reduces the revenue that flows to the supplier and thus reduces the number of suppliers who would be interested in listing a service on the platform. A low commission – or even a negative commission, where the company subsidises the supplier by transferring more to the supplier than the buyer paid, making up the difference with debt or cash from other operations – will increase the revenue per transaction and increase the number of suppliers who elect to join the platform.

Changes to marketing can be made faster than changes to commission. Moreover, marketing changes will not anger existing customers (just slow the arrival of new customers), whereas changes to commission (especially if the commission that the company is taking during the transition is increasing) might anger suppliers.

This challenge of imbalance is a problem that is unique to platforms. A standard company with a linear business model – build, sell, collect the payment – can make as many goods as efficiently as possible that it can sell at a profit. Platforms, in contrast, do not make anything. Their function is to connect buyers and sellers. This change in function introduces new measures for efficiency, where waste is now defined as too many people on one side of the platform and not enough people on the other.

This problem is especially vexing and damaging when the platform is small, and just starting to gain traction and awareness in the marketplace. It cannot afford to attract customers to the platform only to disappoint them so that they leave, perhaps forever. This undermines the platform's network effect and slows its growth. Once a platform gets large and starts to dominate a market sector, this problem of imbalance recedes, in part because customers – buyers or sellers – have nowhere else to go. This is the subject of the following section.

First mover advantage

The "first mover advantage" is a theory that the first company to offer a new product and to solve a customer's problems will dominate the market for all time. This is a myth. As we discussed in Chapter 3, Christensen's disruptive innovation was built on the observation that big dominant companies eventually lose their position to a smaller competitor.

However, platform companies that harness the network effect can dominate a market for an extended period just by being first. This is why this chapter is included in a book on innovation: innovators that build a multi-sided marketplace can push almost all other companies out the way for years – maybe even decades – at a time.

Why can't new entrants jump in and win in industries that allow the network effect? Because when they arrive, these new entrants have a smaller network. They don't have as many users, which means that they're already behind on the curve for the network effect. They cannot create enough value that would jump them ahead of the incumbent for the network effect, at least not organically.

Let's take Facebook as an example. Its 2 billion users create an enormous amount of interesting content (and an even larger amount of uninteresting content) that attracts readers to the website. Facebook itself did not write any of this content. Facebook does not own any cats and does not post any picture of cats on its page. Instead, users post cat pictures, which (for some reason) millions of other people find fascinating.

In 2014, two innovators launched Ello as a competitor to Facebook. It flopped. It had no content in comparison with Facebook. And to create enough content internally to achieve parity with the content that Facebook offered, it would have had to spend millions of dollars on writers and photographers and cats. Within two years, the company pivoted away from peer-to-peer social networking.

This is why innovators seeking impact must consider a platform business model: it is one of the most efficient ways to deliver impactful value to customers.

Network monopolies

Because the first mover advantage is true for platform companies, it is inevitable that many turn into network monopolies. They suffer from no competitive pressure on their prices, which means that they can raise their prices if desired. (If the platform relies on revenue from advertising, it will increase the number of ads that each person sees, simply because it can.) As the company's prices go up, so does its profitability.

Monopolists might also allow product quality to decline. Perhaps the filters for harmful postings fail to keep pace. Or maybe the company is less than rigorous in protecting customer data. "Mistakes" become more common because the company has more customers and more data, and therefore more issues that might require scrutiny for quality. Moreover, unlike for a smaller company, these "mistakes" are unlikely to be fatal for a network monopolist. The company's size and momentum will propel it over the rocks.

Paradoxically, platform companies that seek to become a network monopolist must first spend heavily to grow their networks. Costs far exceed revenues, requiring substantial injections of money, typically from investors with deep pockets who understand the potentially explosive growth that a first mover platform company might achieve. Most platform companies have a hockey stick growth model (see Chapter 6).

Although the first mover advantage is real, many markets inhabited by mature platforms have evolved not into a single monopolist but instead into a stable duopoly, where two players survive. The rest of the competition withers. These two players eventually realise that they will not be able to easily demolish the competition through continued growth, and so they revert to monopolistic-like practices, where they cease a price war and instead slowly raise prices in tacit collusion.

Witness Uber. In most of its markets, it holds a monopoly position over the region's ride-hailing services. In China where Uber was clearly in second place, the company retreated and ceded business to Didi Kaudi (which was formed by a merger of smaller ride players in reaction to Uber's entry). In many markets, Uber still faces stiff competition, like Lyft in US cities, BlaBla in France, Ola in India, and Grab in Southeast Asia. Competition is so fierce in disputed markets, with players losing millions of dollars every day, because the prize for supremacy is so large.

Power of network monopolies

Regulators have battled monopolies for decades. They broke up Ma Bell. They punished Microsoft over its exclusion of Netscape and scrutinised Facebook's "free basics" over fears of monopolistic practices. As platform companies become more prevalent and powerful, regulators are likely to attempt an intervention again. However, the case is harder to make and even harder to solve.

Many network monopolies – Facebook, Google Search and YouTube to name three – rely on revenue from advertising. Customers do not pay a fee to participate in the platform. The platforms are "free", provided that users are willing to look at ads and submit to the sale of their data. The standard signal of a monopoly – extraordinarily high prices – do not apply to these platforms. So regulators must rely on or invent new definitions of monopolies. And the standard regulatory reaction to monopolies – forced price controls – are irrelevant when the price is $0.

Network monopolists also grew because customers saw the value of joining the platform and voluntarily opted in. Nobody forced users to join Facebook. And their survival and standard of living will not be appreciably diminished if they voluntary leave Facebook. This is different to monopolies that control the supply of water, electricity, cellular connectivity or petroleum.

Finally, the most aggressive reaction from regulators – to force a company to divide into smaller pieces and to allow competition to enter their markets – would destroy customer value. Imagine if regulators broke Facebook into separate North American and European companies. All the users of Facebook who joined in order to connect with friends across the ocean would lose value.

In summary, there is no obvious control to network monopolies by regulators. Perhaps the only true check on monopolistic power will emerge from innovations by other companies who find new ways beyond multi-sided platforms to create and deliver value to customers.

An understanding of network monopolies helps innovators understand both the potential end stage of their platform and the possible reactions from regulators.

Risks of disintermediation

The platform as an innovative way to create and deliver value to the customer is not a perfect tool. It has several flaws with different degrees of severity and nuance.[4] In this section, we will tackle two of them: disintermediation and the reaction from the companies that were already in the industry before the platform arrived.

Imagine that you have created a platform where buyers and sellers find each other inside the marketplace. Everything about the match is perfect: the right offer at the right place at the right time. Everyone is happy. However, instead of finalising the transaction on and through the platform, they find a way to communicate outside the platform so that the buyer can pay the seller directly. If the platform relies on commission to generate revenue, the platform is "leaking" revenue to these customers who have bypassed its payment system. You created value but did not generate revenues to cover your costs or to make a profit.

For instance, someone searching for an airline flight might use Expedia to search for the lowest fare, and then jump directly to the airline's own website to book the ticket. Expedia did its job: it provided clear coordination of many buyers and sellers of airline travel. However, Expedia was unable to collect any commission-based revenue for that service.

There are several avenues by which platform companies can tackle the problem of disintermediation. In many instances, platform innovators may decide to ignore it if the loss of revenue is trivial. Why solve a problem if the cure is worse than the disease? If only a small percentage of visitors to Expedia elect to jump directly to a single airline's site, then Expedia should elect to overlook the behaviour.

A second option is to charge an up-front amount for the service with a subscription fee (see Chapter 6), creating an intersection between two types of innovations: subscriptions and platforms. Match.com, a dating site that connects people looking for companionship, uses this approach, charging a monthly membership fee. Relying on subscriptions is feasible only for platform companies that already have a reputation for successful customer experiences because they have demonstrated repeatedly that buyers and sellers can find what they are looking for. A subscription is not recommended for companies that have yet to establish a large network because they will not yet have a reputation for successful connections.

Some platforms try to disallow direct communication between buyer and seller. This can be done by hiding the identity and contact information of buyers and sellers. Airbnb overcame disintermediation by building its own messaging service that precluded (or at least complicated) the ability for buyers and sellers to converse or transact outside the platform.

The platform company might also reinforce the value of paying the commission or subscription with complementary services. For example, Airbnb provides insurance and escrow services only to people who keep their transaction on the platform.

More radically, platforms can go in the opposite direction: reducing the dependence on commissions with complementary services that carry their own fees that cannot be easily bypassed. For example, Hooves.dk, a platform to help horse owners find multiple horse riders, found that almost all its customers bypassed its commission. Instead, it made the connection between owner and rider free to everyone, and then charged a fee for people who wanted professional photographs and another fee for people who used a scheduling tool that coordinated all the activities and records for the horse between the owner, riders, veterinarians and other vendors and stakeholders. The company's offer to "create a team around your horse" generates historical data that discourages disintermediation. By engaging multiple members of a team, the company harnessed the network effect by increasing the value of the service as more people join the team and the platform.

Reactions from incumbents

The theory of disruptive innovation suggests that smaller companies that solve a customer's problem with an innovation at a dramatically lower price will eventually topple most large companies. A platform is just such an innovation. Companies with traditional, linear business models recognise that they do not enjoy the network effect. The entrance of a new company that harnesses the network effect with a platform poses a serious, potentially lethal threat. These incumbents have many different strategies to repel these new entrants. Defending against innovative new entrants benefits from anticipating what those incumbents might attempt.

The law

The first defence for incumbents is the law. A company can secure legal ownership for its idea through patents, trademarks, service marks and copyrights. This allows it to erect barriers in as many ways as possible so that a new platform venture cannot legally use the ideas, designs or processes the incumbents own. Intellectual property protection depends on enforcement by governments to reduce competition intentionally. Luckily, the innovation of a platform to create and deliver value is not by itself considered protectable intellection property. Attempts to do so have been defeated. For example, Amazon attempted to put a patent on its "One Click" checkout mechanism to allow buyers to quickly purchase an item. The US courts did not allow this claim.

If existing laws are not sufficient, incumbents often endeavour to grab the ears of legislators to create new laws. This is called "regulatory capture". In most economies, companies with traditional business models are those that have historically had the money, power and lobbyists to control the mechanisms of government. Platforms have a few retorts to this manoeuvre.

1. **Lower costs.** First, they usually lower costs for consumers, which earns the appreciation of consumers. In representative democracies, these consumers vote. Legislators are hesitant to hurt their own constituents.

2. **Withholding resources.** Incumbents can also combat platforms by withholding resources. For example, many luxury clothing brands like Gucci refuse to allow marketplaces like Amazon to sell their products. This gambit can be self-defeating. Companies that reduce customer access to their products eventually lose to companies that are more aggressive about marketing. Moreover, powerful platforms create their own brands and connections to customers. Customers select Uber for transportation; they no longer consider the brand of the car that arrives to transport them. Ford, Toyota and

other manufacturers have been pushed to the back seat in customer minds.

3. **If you can't beat them ...** Incumbents can react to the entry to platforms into their market by innovating themselves. After losing market share to Amazon, retailers Walmart and Target both started their own online marketplaces that invite buyers and sellers who do not already participate in their physical stores.

These incumbents can follow all the processes and trajectories already described in this book to find their own innovations that solve customer problems even more suitably than the upstart platforms. Methods such as design thinking, the blue ocean strategy, the lean start-up method and subscriptions are all tools available to incumbents.

The platform generation

At the turn of the millennium, we entered the digital age. Children born after the year 2000 are "digital natives" such that most of their social, school and business interactions occur online. We are now living in the platform age, where more and more of our purchases and experiences involve online platforms. People born after 2015 are "platform natives" because they might never own a car or house. They might never visit a supermarket. They might never read a newspaper – on paper or online. Instead, they will use Uber for local transport, Airbnb for lodging, Amazon for purchases, and Facebook for information. Innovators who seek impact must consider platforms, either as a business model to adopt or a business model to supplement. This consideration might involve design thinking or the lean start-up method and could involve innovative pricing or an alternative use of data. This latter opportunity is the subject of the next chapter.

8

Data-driven innovation

Of the many things that make China both fascinating and frustrating for visitors is the refusal of taxi drivers to accept forms of payment that are conventional elsewhere. The problem repeats when it is time for coffee or lunch. Even credit cards are seldom accepted. Cash hardly ever is. Instead, merchants insist that payments be completed using the mobile apps from WeChat Pay or Alipay, the dominant contactless financial services companies.

Everybody in China uses their phone to send and receive money. Whereas foreigners struggle with it, this widespread innovation makes for a convenient shopping experience for both the merchant and their customers. Yet its greatest impact is the further innovations it makes possible. The constant flow of data informs Alipay's parent company, Ant Group (or "Ant"), on how well each merchant is doing, whether their wares are competitively priced, and whether the business owners are credit-worthy. Equipped with this futuristic due diligence, they can disburse small business loans in minutes and without human intervention.

Having access to billions of transactions also allows payment companies to find correlations in consumer behaviours that elude even the most attentive of humans. For example, Ant identified a group of users who spent more than others on fixing their mobile phone screens. These same users also spent more money than others on tight jeans. Ant now offers innovative screen insurance targeted at females who wear tight jeans.

As digital technologies become ubiquitous, we are getting better at capturing data, making sense of it, and using it to power the two types of innovation we cover in this chapter:

- to create or deliver value with clever data analytics, like Ant's automatic lending
- to leverage data to create new value propositions, like the screen insurance.[1]

From raw data to intelligent decisions

In 1992, data analyst Karen Heath found that men shopping for nappies at Walmart were also likely to buy beer. Accordingly, sales for both items increased when they were placed near each other.[2] This shows the power of data analytics to support decisions that lead to increased business performance. Heath created value with just one correlation of the spending habits of one consumer across two items.

In the early 2000s Andrew Pole helped retailer Target develop a 'pregnancy prediction' score for its clients. Based on products like unscented lotions and zinc supplements that mothers-to-be start buying in their second trimester, Target could estimate the due date and send perfectly timed coupons. When mothers went to Target to redeem their nappy coupons, they also shopped for groceries. The new data-driven focus on expecting mothers resulted in a 50% revenue growth in eight years.[3]

Even the most data-driven decisions in the world of physical retail are limited to a few dozen data points. Online retail is not similarly constrained. E-commerce giants, like Alibaba in China or Zalando in Europe, know not only what items customers purchase but also hundreds of other demographic and behavioural data, such as what other items they viewed, how much time they spent on the site, and whether they reacted to promotions or product reviews. Such data, systematically collected from millions of consumers over time, power algorithms to predict what items customers might want to buy next, based on what similar customers purchased in the past. The algorithm can then automatically make recommendations to increase sales.

Make my data BIG

Big data refers to datasets that are too large and complex to be processed with traditional analytics techniques. These datasets are defined by three key features: the 3 Vs.

1. **Volume.** The amount of data gathered and stored influences its ability to generate valuable insights. For example, Dubai International Airport collects over 30 billion data points every year in its real-time analytics platform – *for baggage alone*. A single jet engine generates more than 20 terabytes of data per hour of flight.

2. **Velocity.** The speed at which data are gathered and processed affects the ability to generate actionable insights. For example, whereas sales data from the various restaurants in a chain can be collected at the end of each day of trading, data from traffic sensors must be processed

in real time to reduce congestion; a delay of even a few minutes would make the data ineffective and possibly even counterproductive.

3. **Variety.** The nature and type of data determine the ability to generate novel insights. Big datasets include very heterogenous data points, ranging from video streams to geolocation, from spending habits to demographic data. For example, health monitoring systems use data as diverse as body temperature, heart rate, respiratory rate, chest sounds, blood pressure, step count, location, accelerometer and gyroscope data.

Traditional data analytics techniques were not designed to cope effectively with such volume, velocity or variety. Enter a new generation of data analytics techniques, fit for the world of big data.

Intelligence turns artificial

Traditional data analysis relies on humans to assemble the data, to determine what questions to ask of the data, and to interpret the results. Not anymore. With large datasets and outputs affected by dozens of factors, human intelligence is at a loss. The prevalent approach today, machine learning (ML), lets computers uncover correlations between data with or without human supervision.

After millions of users tagged "get rich quick" emails from alleged Nigerian princes as "spam", Gmail's algorithm learned to recognise them as undesired emails and now automatically sends them to the junk folder. This common approach to ML is called *supervised learning*, where algorithms are based on examples provided initially by humans. For example, when a photo of a person is accompanied by a human-generated tag with that person's name, the algorithm learns to associate the two. It learns the same way to associate songs with their genre and translate texts into other languages. Each time algorithms analyse a new object, they become more accurate.

In the example of Ant Group, humans did not look for correlations between spending on screens and tight jeans. Instead, they let algorithms cluster consumers depending on commonalities across many variables. Since no human-generated tag is required, this approach is called *unsupervised learning*. Algorithms parse the data and identify patterns humans cannot easily spot. Using this same technique, your bank can quickly decide whether your latest credit card purchase belonged in the group of legitimate transactions or fraudulent ones.

A variant of unsupervised learning is *reinforcement learning*. After specifying the rules of the game and the standards of successful performance, algorithms learn how to succeed by trial and error. Unlike the previous two techniques, reinforcement learning does not require large sets of historical data, because the algorithms generate their own data by trial and error.

As we increasingly rely on algorithms that learn on their own, one of the techniques used to improve their performance is *deep learning*. Deep-learning algorithms analyse features of datasets one at a time, developing deeper and deeper layers of analysis, hence the name. This technique can be applied to each of the three learning styles above.

ML algorithms can now perform actions that *appear* to be

Concept

ARTIFICIAL INTELLIGENCE

Algorithms that make decisions, which appear to be intelligent by human standards

Examples: classifying emails as spam, predicting search keywords, translating between languages, suggesting relevant ads, recommending books and movies, understanding voice commands, playing chess and other games, driving autonomous vehicles, optimising traffic lights, suggesting driving routes, predicting customer churn

Implementation

MACHINE LEARNING

Algorithms that identify patterns among large amounts of data (i.e., associate input with outputs) and learn (i.e., their performance improves as they process more data over time)

Techniques

SUPERVISED LEARNING	UNSUPERVISED LEARNING	REINFORCEMENT LEARNING
Algorithms identify patterns in data following human guidance	**Algorithms identify patterns in data without following human guidance**	**Algorithms identify patterns in data through trial and error**
Examples: recommending books and movies, classifying emails as spam	Examples: driving autonomous vehicles, predicting search keywords	Examples: optimising traffic lights, playing chess and other games

DEEP LEARNING

Algorithms identify patterns in data by analysing features in sequential steps and not all at once. It's used for all three learning techniques.

Example: deep unsupervised learning

Figure 5. Overview of artificial intelligence
Source: A. Lanteri, *Clever: The Six Strategic Drivers for the Fourth Industrial Revolution* (Lioncrest, 2019)

intelligent by human standards and so have earned the title of artificial intelligence (AI). Figure 5 depicts how all these ideas are related to each other.

Artificial intelligence in the service of innovation

Data analytics allows the optimisation of a range of decisions, like how many sweaters of different sizes and colours to stock based on predicted aggregate demand, or what ads to run based on the resulting sales. These rough population-level estimates were possible even before big data, but large datasets combined with intelligent algorithms now make greater accuracy possible.

Netflix understands its viewers so well that each enjoys a uniquely customised experience. In 2013, it stated that "there are 33 million different versions of Netflix" because it had 33 million subscribers.[4] Netflix constantly tests different recommendations, sometimes even developing different trailers for different users, to gauge what content works best. With data suggesting that customers exhibit different viewing behaviour depending on day, time and location, Netflix now has more versions than it has subscribers in its attempts to innovate how its customers choose their entertainment and find value in the service.

In 2012, Amazon filed a patent for a system of anticipatory delivery. Amazon can ship an item to individual customers, or at least ensure they are in transit, even before purchase. This way it can deliver within hours of a confirmed order, living up to the demanding expectations of its Prime premium subscription.

The Economist suggested that "data is the new oil", supporting business models in the digital age, just as oil powered the industrial era.[5] AI is the engine running on this fuel.

Three tasks fit for AI

To understand how AI can be employed to create value, it helps to think of the three key tasks it excels at.[6]

1. **Classification**. AI can categorise new inputs as belonging to predefined categories. For example, Gmail can determine whether an email is spam, promotional or social. Mastercard can determine if a transaction is fraudulent.

2. **Predicting future outcomes** by estimating the next data in a sequence. For example, AI can determine whether a merchant will default on a loan. It can forecast airline bookings at different rates depending on consumer sentiment and weather.

3. **Creating novel data**. For example, AI can generate new taxi routes depending on real-time traffic information, even if no one has already discovered the route. In 2020, the *Guardian* newspaper ran an op-ed that was written by AI, using minimal input and requiring less editing than most human-written pieces would.[7]

This kind of advanced performance is more readily relatable to your business and ours than it may appear. For example, we know many professors who would like to use AI to grade lengthy students' assignments. The algorithm would scan an essay and *classify* it as a B- or C+, accurately and reliably, saving our colleagues precious time. Professors could also use students' behaviour to *predict* their grades. For example, one of our colleagues elaborated a system that reliably predicted the final grade of undergraduate students based on the frequency of access to the online repository where readings and assignments are stored, as well as the amount of time they spend on it. Alessandro used this insight on several occasions as an early warning system for students at risk of underperforming. He then reached out to those students early in the term and provided additional support when there was still time.

Education would greatly benefit from learning journeys customised to each individual student – for example, based on their preferred learning styles, and recent performance in other courses. AI-powered systems could create such learning journeys in a way similar to taxi routes. With just one application for each of AI's main capabilities, we could turn professors into super-professors.

AI gives us humans superpowers of sorts, by improving our performance in the tasks we value. If you had a system to classify new inputs quickly and accurately, to make accurate predictions, or even to create brand new sources of value, what would you use it for? What superpower would you seek?

Use of digital data in the physical world

Whereas online retailers are ideally positioned to capture data, brick and mortar stores are quickly catching up with the benefits of harvesting data. Sensors and hidden cameras with visual recognition capabilities track shoppers' movements; virtual trolleys connected to cashier-less checkout systems match individual shoppers with their spending habits. In 2018, Walmart filed a patent for a trolley equipped with biometric sensors to track customers' heart rates and stress levels to improve their shopping experience.

Physical stores are also increasingly integrated with multi-channel distribution systems. With its acquisition of Whole Foods, Amazon gained access to conveniently located fresh products as well as fulfilment centres closer to customers. Amazon's AI system can predict the demand for products at new stores by extrapolating from hundreds of different variables in nearby cities.

Multiple points for value creation

Clever data analytics create value for many different parts of a company beyond just customer features. AI-powered robots locate, pick and transport each of the thousands of items in the warehouses of British supermarket Ocado. This increases the speed of fulfilment. As soon as these items are packed and dropped on a conveyor belt, another AI-powered system checks the weight of each package against the items it should contain. Any mismatch is flagged for manual verification by a human, thus reducing the cost of quality control.

Beside executing standard routines differently to increase efficiency, AI enriches processes to incorporate data never used before. The hospitality giant Marriott developed a dynamic pricing automation, which combines real-time data from a variety of sources (like local and global economic data, events and weather reports) with internal metrics (like average occupancy rate, gross operating profit per room and reservation trends). Marriott adjusts its pricing strategy accordingly and proactively. For example, if a consumer checks availability at a beach resort from a location where it is currently raining, the system can increase the rates. This data also helps optimise staffing decisions at each property.

Machine learning vs machine creativity

As we've discussed, innovation involves identifying needs, generating possible solutions, testing them, and using feedback to refine them. Machine learning is extremely efficient at just that.

With price tags as high as $15 million per episode, shooting a TV series is a capital-intensive business. Before committing such resources for a new series with uncertain viewer demand, producers circulate pilot episodes to test public reactions. Even so, the success rate for new shows is less than 40%, because pilot testing is an imperfect system to collect information. Netflix's original shows have an 80% success rate, without pilots. The world-famous series *House of Cards* was developed based on previous viewers' ratings of other shows. The theme, the lead actor and the director had already been validated by millions of users. In this way, data analytics inspires and improves innovation.

However, this still comes short of inventing something new. This is the realm of machine creativity. One of the first and most famous displays of machine creativity took place in early March 2016 at Seoul's Four Seasons Hotel. Lee Sedol, 18 times world champion and widely considered one of the most talented human players of Go, a strategy game vastly more complex than chess, was playing against AlphaGo, a Go computer program developed by Google's DeepMind. At first considered a mistake by Go experts, AlphaGo's 19th move, the 37th in the game, was unlike any move ever made by a human player in the game's 2,500-year history. It was also the move that paved the way to a historic defeat for the human champion.

In a similar way, algorithms trained on large databases of existing molecules and their properties can explore the novemdecillion (10^{60}) different drug-like molecules believed to exist to develop new treatments, a feat beyond any human. In engineering, generative software can quickly suggest multiple different ways to solve a problem, based on dozens of design parameters, such as materials, manufacturing techniques and cost constraints. Experts emphasise that AI does not only process large amounts of data quickly but also identifies solutions that humans would not envision. It thinks differently.

When it comes to creativity, AI still has limitations compared with humans. Humans must remain in the driver's seat, both to ensure common sense and sound ethics. However, in an age of volatile and competitive markets and increasingly costly and risky innovations, the way innovation is managed is ripe for innovation as well. AI's enormous cost advantages in processing information make it an obvious area to look for solutions.

Artificial hypothesis testing

In Chapter 5, we discussed the importance of testing hypotheses to validate innovation. Data-rich, artificial replicas of real-world items and places, called digital twins, eliminate the need for physical experimentation while optimising performance under different conditions. For example, Ireland's public mail service, An Post, collaborated with consulting company Accenture to develop digital twins of sorting centres and vehicles to experiment with new processes and delivery routes to optimise timeliness and throughput.

Similarly, Siemens uses digital twins to test different wind and climate conditions on its railway coaches, saving costs and reducing testing times by half. Digital twins are software replicas of physical entities – their physical twins – like assets, devices, places and processes. Modelled on reality, but isolated from it, digital twins have the same properties as the physical twin and are continuously updated with data from connected sensors. They are used to understand, predict and optimise performance of their physical counterparts to achieve improved business outcomes.

Digital twins also overcome limitations where testing may be unfeasible or unethical. For example, digital twins of real cities can experiment with new traffic systems without interfering with real world vehicles. Philips uses a digital replica of the human heart to evaluate different treatment options before recommending a therapy.

Using AI to innovate the process of innovation

In the early 1960s, Gordon Moore, a co-founder of microprocessor manufacturer Intel, observed that every 18–24 months, computer processors become half the size while doubling in computing power. The accelerating rate at which more power fits smaller processors, referred to as Moore's Law, powered technological advances that led us to the digital age. Today, to double chip density, research teams need to be 18 times bigger than in the 1970s. Progress is therefore slowing down. Similar declines in research productivity occurred in drug discovery and seed innovation. The same rate of innovation can be maintained only with increasing research investments, or with better processes to transform data into validated insights.

Pioneering experiments in computational chemistry expect to develop a "self-driving laboratory" capable of inventing new materials with improved chemical structures and properties at the incredible rate of one per hour. Algorithms can learn the properties of different chemical compounds to generate new chemical structures. Robotic arms can operate pipettes and other machines to automate lab testing. AI accelerates "retrosynthesis", figuring out backwards the process required to synthesise new materials. The large amounts of data produced by the experiments are then fed back to keep the algorithms learning and progressively creating a library of new materials. So far, the materials created contain unique properties optimised for applications as diverse as electrolytes to increase battery performance, inexpensive organic solar cells, compounds that absorb pollution and chromophores used in cancer surgery.

An AlphaGo moment in pharmaceuticals may not be far away. It has already happened in biology, where AlphaFold has made dramatic strides towards solving protein folding, a grand challenge of over five decades. Understanding proteins' shapes and their functions is fundamental to solving problems such as treating diseases or breaking down industrial waste. With such promise of impact, this new ML-powered approach to innovation is poised to be the greatest economic impact of AI.

While some of these exciting examples may seem far-fetched, they serve as a warning for possible incoming revolutions in your current market, though perhaps not coming from your current competitors, as well as a direction to scout groundbreaking opportunities to innovate.

Internet of things

The data that companies collect, the smart devices that gather such data and the systems used to automate and optimise decisions constitute an internet of things (IoT) that connects the physical and the digital worlds. In Californian almond orchards, every 30 minutes moisture sensors determine whether micro-sprinklers should water each individual tree, which side of its trunk, and whether fertiliser should be added. This ensures optimal hydration for the tree and maximises yield, while reducing the consumption of critically scarce water by 20%.

Elsewhere, the IoT is transforming the way data are gathered and processed to automate smart homes, factories, infrastructures, and cities. A promising aspect of the IoT relates to machine-to-machine, such as the boiler in your house having sensors connected to the internet and exchanging data with other databases up on the web. The data exchange can heat your house when it knows you have left your workplace; it can also set a higher temperature if the internet weather station says that a cold front is coming in.

The IoT is accelerating new platform ventures. It's being used with the trucking business, for instance, using GPS to track the movement of long-haul trucks to ensure that drivers are staying safe, adhering to regulations about how many hours they can drive, ensuring that refrigerated goods stay cold, and notifying warehouses at the destination that a shipment is about to arrive. The advisory company IDC estimates that 60% of world GDP will be digitised by 2022.

In effect, the IoT helps companies customise their value proposition. You're no longer necessarily just part of a customer segment. It's possible for companies to target you individually and customise their offerings to just you. This is not unique to the sharing economy but it certainly is finding new outlets and new value there.

The IoT is creating new markets every day. Uber Eats is an example of a company that is now not just tracking the person who likes a ride but is also tracking a bag of food or other types of shipment. The internet of things is the technology that is underneath the ability for the sharing economy to make markets and match buyers with sellers.

Ultimately, sharing ventures disintermediate traditional companies, but ironically, they also "re-intermediate" the connection between customers and the value they are searching to find. Hotels are in trouble because of Airbnb but at the same time, Airbnb becomes a new intermediary, connecting travellers with values. It can do this thanks to the sharing of data on buyers and sellers through all the interconnected sensors and data collected from the IoT.

Disintermediation typically is good for consumers. It reduces the links in the value chain, which means that consumers can go more directly to suppliers. It is bad for the venture that is being disintermediated. If you're in the travel agency business right now, you're having a terrible time and it's only going to get worse. On the flip side, re-intermediation with ventures and the sharing economy where they capture lots of different data, that's good for the venture. It is good for a sharing venture to collect, hold and hopefully leverage this data.

Blockchains and the internet of value

The unique features of data – that it is intangible and can be freely duplicated – are also a challenge. If you want to send money to anyone, you have to rely on several intermediaries to do so for you. Your bank first verifies that you own the funds. It then instructs a further intermediary, like SWIFT, which coordinates the money transfer to the recipient bank. This latter will eventually credit the money to a specific account. This process often takes days and entails costs. It compromises confidentiality, by making all the third parties privy to your identity and the recipient's. But it's also a good thing, helping to prevent money laundering and other financial crimes.

Disintermediating exchanges of value, particularly online, has proved difficult. If you could simply send someone a digital message indicating that you want them to have some digital money, without any independent verification, you could easily copy and paste the same message and send it to many other recipients. In other words, you could "double spend" (or triple or quadruple). If everyone was able to multiply money this way, such money would quickly become worthless. Enter cryptocurrencies and the blockchain.

A blockchain is a ledger that records in chronological order all the transactions that have ever been executed within a system. Most cryptocurrencies have a ledger that details every transaction ever completed since the creation of the currency. So that each individual unit of the currency, called a token, can be traced back to the moment of its creation, through each transaction, across multiple owners and wallets. In other words, if you have a bitcoin or another token and you spend it, this will be publicly recorded and you will not be able to double spend it. In so doing, your identity and that of the recipient are protected by a pseudonym.

The idea of a blockchain was first described by the elusive inventor of bitcoin, Satoshi Nakamoto, in 2008. The name itself comes from the bitcoin system, where bitcoin transactions are not individually settled, but grouped and processed in *blocks* of multiple transactions. To make the system more resistant to alterations, each block also contains a unique cryptographic number (a *hash*) that refers to the previous block. In this way, each block is linked to the previous and the following one, effectively creating a *chain*. A blockchain is ultimately, and perhaps unsurprisingly, a chain of blocks.

The blockchain beyond cryptocurrencies

Numerous applications of blockchain beyond payments and across industries are becoming commonplace. The blockchain is now recognised as a general-purpose technology, considered equivalent to a new internet for its potential to become the technological infrastructure for big data. Thanks to its cryptographic protocols and mechanisms for validating transactions (called *consensus*), blockchains allow value to be exchanged online and without intermediaries, potentially creating a veritable "internet of value".

Beside keeping tabs on the owners of cryptocurrencies, blockchain ledgers can record the owners of any number of other assets. They could host digital land registries where each parcel of land is uniquely assigned to a token. So, the owner of the token owns the land. Tokens can also track rights to intellectual property like recorded music or digital paintings. For digital tokens used as currency, it is essential that each coin is identical to every other, just like a dollar bill is equivalent to any other dollar bill. We call such assets "fungible", meaning that they can be replaced by other identical assets. On the contrary, these new applications of blockchain consists in assets that are unique and non-fungible. Hence, we call them non-fungible tokens (NFTs). For example, *The Economist* raised more than $400,000 for charity by selling the NFTs corresponding to its digital cover "Down the rabbit hole". If you bought one of those tokens, you would own a share of that cover.

NFTs may seem just fanciful novelties. Yet they have increasingly valuable applications. For example, they can be associated with luxury and collectors' items, to prevent counterfeiting. When purchasing rare wine bottles, for example, collectors could acquire the corresponding token, therefore simplifying the contract and the transaction. This way they could also verify that the seller legitimately owns an authentic rare bottle. In a similar way, one could own a fraction of a painting or another asset, which may be too expensive to buy in its entirety and too complicated to sell when necessary. Finally, NFTs could create a connection between the physical and the digital world. NFTs linked to physical products could store data about the origin of a product, the raw materials employed and their origin. The entire supply chain can become digitised this way, and so defective products could be detected earlier, and authenticity could be proven.

Transforming to seize digital value

These fascinating digital technologies have the potential to create great value for an organisation. However, they cannot be deployed in isolation. They require a suitable style of decision-making, leadership approach and more generally a digital culture to fulfil their promise. For most organisations this entails a transformative effort.

The first stage of the transformation consists in converting information which previously existed or was handled in paper form into digital data. This is *digitisation*. For example, to open a bank account you may have walked to the local branch and filled in a form. When Alessandro last attempted this, he was sent away with the instructions to download an app and complete a digital form. He was later summoned to meet in person with a bank officer who had printed out the application. The bank had not yet gone through the next stage, *digitalisation*, or the transformation of the work processes. The result was frustration and inefficiency. Simply paying lip service to digital opportunities backfires and destroys value.

Although digital transformation is not the same as innovation, the two often progress in sync and require similar mindsets, culture and processes. Both aim at new sources of value, by improving customer outcomes, operational processes, or both. For example, clothing companies achieve cost efficiencies by reducing inventories, using data to predict demand and so make purchase, design and manufacturing decisions not based on habit or seniority, but in an entirely new way. Indeed, *digital transformation is about people and culture* much more than it is about digital technology.

Four tiers of digital value

To navigate the many ways to create value with digital transformation, it helps to consider four tiers, each of which harvests and analyses data internally or externally and offers a unique strategic advantage.[8]

- **Tier One**. Data are generated and used internally to achieve operational efficiencies. For example, the car manufacturer Ford has deployed a combination of the IoT, AI, augmented reality and extended reality to perform automated inspection of paint jobs and so reduce defects in its factories.

- **Tier Two**. Data are generated externally, but used internally, to achieve advanced operational efficiencies. For example, construction machines are equipped with sensors that help heavy equipment manufacturer Caterpillar to determine how they are used at the clients' construction sites and optimise the motors and other features for each given use.

- **Tier Three**. Data are generated and used externally to offer new services. The sensors installed on GE's jet engines generate a constant stream of data that allow the real-time optimisation of fuel consumption, benefiting the client. GE is paid for the fuel savings in addition to the price received for the engine itself.

- **Tier Four**. Data are generated and used externally to offer new services as in Tier Three, but through a digital platform. Peloton makes internet-connected home exercise equipment. The data generated from the stationary bikes and treadmills help match users with external personal trainers and collect such user-interaction data to facilitate further exchanges with third-party providers.

Although there is no right or wrong tier of digital transformation a company should strive for, Tier One is increasingly a must. The urgency of collecting and using data to create value seems hard to deny.

But if you are not doing this already, where should you start?

Start with quick wins

There are dozens of different ways in which data can be used to create value in an existing organisation or for a brand-new project, but there is no one-size-fits-all ranking of priority. Instead, there are guiding principles that are worth exploring.

Start by listing a few opportunities to use data and perhaps AI to improve performance. For example, you can think about a usual bottleneck you encounter or one of the main key performance indicators (KPIs) where your team underperforms. Remember, these opportunities can be based on the two types of task at which AI excels: classification and prediction.

Then classify the opportunities you've identified above, using two dimensions. The first dimension is the strategic value the opportunity can create. Consider any of the benefits, which might include reduced costs, increased revenues, improved service quality, better overall performance, lower chance of mistakes, avoidance of boring or repetitive tasks, accelerated time to market, easier access to distribution or greater stakeholder satisfaction. The greater the strategic value of the opportunity, the more it should be prioritised. Yet this is not enough.

The second dimension concerns the complexity of pursuing the opportunity. Consider how many different data points are required and whether you already have such data or whether you need to collect them from scratch. Do other parties need to be involved in data collection and, if so, would they benefit from the data or would they just consider it a waste of time? How difficult or expensive is it to access these data and ensure their quality? The less complex a project, the more it should be prioritised.

You should initially look for a quick win. Such choice will also diminish internal resistance from others in your organisation. Moreover, when a project like this succeeds, it is likely that others will want to achieve something similar; a quick win is a great way to get started on a digital transformation trajectory.[9]

For example, Amarillo College in Texas started with a data analytics project to understand why students dropped out and to improve graduation rates. It found out that the leading causes included a range of financial challenges, from food and housing insecurity to the demands of being a primary caregiver and the challenges associated with transportation or unexpected expenses.

These data flew in the face of all the conventional wisdom of how colleges should ensure that their students graduate and led to a dramatic innovation of the entire model. Amarillo College now teaches financial management classes, offers access to a food pantry, runs a subsidised daycare centre, and even offers emergency loans for sudden expenses, like car repairs or utility bills. As a result, graduation rates went through the roof and Amarillo College emerged as a new organisation that successfully pursues its mission by making effective decisions driven by data analytics.

This is no Google-like success story. That is exactly the point:

data-driven decisions and innovation are not a prerogative of colossal high-tech corporations. Digital transformation ensures an organisation is future-ready and it continues to create value and deliver impact.

Over the years, founding enterprises as well as teaching and advising companies on digital innovation, it has become evident to us that everyone can use data-driven approaches to create value, albeit doing so does not come intuitively to most people. To get there, one needs to understand the importance of data, which tasks can be best performed using AI, and how it can create value. This is what this chapter is all about.

In the next chapter, we turn to a kind of innovation that expands the definition of value beyond the simply economic: innovation that creates social value.

9

Social innovation

In the middle of the Pacific Ocean, roughly between San Francisco and Hawaii, there is a crossroads of ocean currents that creates a spinning vortex of water. This "gyre" has existed for eons. More recently, small particles of plastic from sources all over the world have become stuck in the vortex. Billions of pieces, some too small for the human eye to see, float in the ocean, disrupting natural patterns of marine line. Whales and fish eat the plastic and die. Sunlight cannot easily penetrate the plastic, causing harmful changes to water composition and algae. The Great Pacific Garbage Patch is estimated to be 620,000 square miles (1.6 million km^2), which is more than twice the size of Texas or Turkey.

There have been attempts to remove these plastic particles with clever technologies. To date, they have failed because the cost of filtering the water is higher than anyone wants to pay. Moreover, the patch is not legally owned by any one country, and the plastic in the patch comes from hundreds of different countries. This is simultaneously everyone's problem and nobody's problem.

Rubbish in the ocean is an illustration of a market failure. There is no single customer who would pay to clean the ocean. The people who would benefit from cleaning the rubbish are too disbursed and diffuse. There is no way to identify exactly how much each person would benefit, and no way to convince these beneficiaries to pay. Concurrently, there is no way to identify each of the contributors to the problem – those who are discarding plastic into the ocean intentionally or mistakenly – and no way to charge them for the harm that they are creating. The ocean is simply too big to monitor. There is as yet no market that would fund this innovation.

Public goods

Economists recognise that there are many types of resource that fall victim to market failures of this kind. These resources share a common trait: they are non-exclusive. There is no easy, cost-effective way to keep people from using as much of the resource as they choose. As a result, there is no way to charge those who benefit from these resources. Oceans, air, lighthouses, public forests and even national defence are examples of goods that cannot selectively forbid people from enjoying the good or service if they elect not to pay.

There is another category of resource where a business can indeed control who uses it, and the customer does indeed benefit from it. However, the use of the product also generates huge benefits for other people, most of whom are not charged a fee. Primary education is an example. By teaching a young child to read and write, not only will that child have access to better jobs, but the education spills over to other aspects of human civilisation. People who are educated are healthier, less likely to get or spread diseases. They are better neighbours and citizens, contributing to public welfare. They are better parents, so their children will be healthier and more productive. This leads to a conundrum: who should pay for primary education? If we conclude that society should pay for at least some of the cost, who do we charge and how much?

Why does this notion of market failure matter to innovation? The processes and trajectories for innovation discussed so far share a common assumption: that supplier and buyer can find a mutually agreeable price such that the supplier can make a profit. In other words, we have assumed until now that there is a functioning market. This chapter describes ways in which innovators can create new, valuable products and services outside functioning markets for the benefit of society.

Why should this matter to innovators? First, because an innovation that relies on the presence of a traditional market might not yet be able to survive in the middle of a market failure. Second and more important is the word "yet" in the preceding sentence. It is possible that clever, impactful innovations with technology, pricing, value creation or value delivery might create a market and revenues when none have existed to date.

These innovations solve wider social and environmental problems that have a less direct connection to revenue generation. Market failures are often the domain of charities or non-profit organisations, which rely on donations or grants to fund their activities, or governments, which use a combination of taxpayers' money and policymaking. These products intend to solve or ameliorate a local or global social or economic challenge: everything from climate change, poverty and racism to deforestation, pollution, illiteracy, inequality or corruption, among others.

The most important message we want to impart is that every world-changing innovation was conceived by someone just like you, who had a vision of impact and needed some clarity about the mechanism to bring that innovation to life. Moreover, every innovation that achieved global impact started by achieving local impact. While you might eventually expect to change the world, you can start by changing the lives of just a few people in just a few ways for the better.

Continuum of profits and social impact

We have introduced this concept of social innovation in juxtaposition to profit-making innovation. In reality, there is no line between social and profitable innovations. Most innovations mix the two along a spectrum. At one end of the continuum, purely commercial companies innovate as the means to generate profits for their own self-interest. Such a company focuses entirely on the market. Its only core principle is to generate economic value for itself. Its customers certainly benefit from innovation (or else they would not buy the product), but they pay market prices. These companies secure initial investment from market-based mechanisms – venture capitalists, banks, or cash from customers. Employees within and suppliers to such a company are also motivated by profit, commanding market prices for their labour and other inputs.

At the other end of the spectrum lie non-profit charities whose innovations endeavour to solve a problem that transcends markets and individual customers. Often these entities exist precisely because a market has failed. Take the example of pollution. No individual company or customer has the power to make an appreciable difference to the problem. And no company or customer would have an outsized profit by addressing the problem. As a result, most companies and customers elect to continue their traditional behaviours that lead to pollution, guaranteeing that the problem endures.

To tackle these society-wide problems, charities rely on income and investment from people who are willing to pay much more than they benefit. For example, donors to charities that are trying to address pollution would only benefit as much as any other person in the society. And yet these individuals are willing to pay an outsized portion of the costs to implement the solution. Their motivation is the mission, not the profit.

However, there is a special breed of hybrid organisations that primarily pursue social value while also ensuring financial viability. Doing so requires a great deal of innovation, to go beyond the traditional models at the two extremes. Think for example of Toms, a shoe company founded in 2006 by Blake Mycoskie that donates one pair of shoes to a child in need for every pair purchased by an affluent customer in the developed world. The business model referred to as "buy one, give one" is now followed by scores of companies selling every type of consumer product. This is one obvious way of combining full market price and charitable donations.

A company's "bottom line" is the last entry in its income statement that reports its profit. The term "double bottom line" marries financial performance with social impact on the expectation that the company is trying both to increase profits and to address a social issue. More recently, the phrase "triple bottom line" adds the expectation that companies make a profit, address social issues and improve the physical environment.

All the lessons and tools in this book about innovation apply to social innovation. People who seek social innovation show the innovator's mindset. They work in organisations that emphasise innovation. They aim for disruptive innovations that change the way that customers choose to solve their problems, hoping that customers will shift from frequently large incumbent companies towards new entrants that offer a dramatically different solution. Social innovators want not only to take market share from these large incumbents, but also to reduce the social or environmental damage that they might accuse these incumbents of making. Social innovators can use ethnography, design thinking, the blue ocean strategy, open innovation and the lean start-up method. They can create social innovations using novel pricing techniques, multi-sided platforms, data and artificial intelligence.

However, social innovators face additional challenges. Their desire to solve multiple issues simultaneously – customer problems, profits, social impact and environmental resilience – creates extra pressure and difficulties. There are several tools that have been specifically designed to help social innovators find successful novel solutions.

Corporate social responsibility

The idea that corporations should contribute to social change originated in the United States in 1953 when Howard Bowen, an American economist, coined the term "corporate social responsibility" (CSR). Many companies interpret this admonishment as a mandate to make their supply chains less environmentally damaging.

The concept caught on when companies like Ben & Jerry's, The Body Shop and outdoor clothing retailer Patagonia attracted vast consumer loyalty and "fandom" because of their commitment to see business as a means both to make money and to solving global problems, but this approach to business is now popular worldwide.

Patagonia manufactures its products with environmentally sustainable materials. In fact, the company has invested into the research and development of new types of recycled cloth that sometimes performs better than its more environmentally impactful predecessors. The company has expanded its CSR efforts beyond supply. It ensures that it pays its employees a liveable wage with generous benefits, resulting in a labour force that is well trained and loyal with low staff turnover. It has added a service to repair old Patagonia products at low prices to solve customer problems, without the unnecessary use of scarce natural resources. The company then donates 1% of its annual revenue from sale to non-profits that improve the preservation and restoration of the natural environment – what it calls an earth tax.

The sum total of these individual incremental innovations is a company that is dramatically distinct from its competitors. Not every innovation that you consider and launch needs to change the world. It is possible that your successive innovations will amplify each other to create an aggregated impact.

These CSR-related innovations have done much more for Patagonia than simply reduce the harm it causes. The company attracts attention, and loyalty, from customers who want not just to solve an immediate problem – keeping warm, with a Patagonia jacket – but also a much larger ethical conundrum – the reduction of pollution and poverty around the world.

The notion of CSR is not without controversy. The mid-20th-century conservative economist Milton Friedman insisted that the sole purpose of corporations was to make money for its stockholders. He railed against the corporate social responsibility movement as a "fundamentally subversive doctrine" and "hypocritical window dressing" to disguise the real value of corporations to make profits. The battle between these two viewpoints continued for several decades. Some corporations launched efforts at CSR, such as supporting an arts organisation or a charity. For example, in 2001, Coca-Cola established the Africa Foundation, which worked to prevent and treat HIV/Aids in Africa; in 2007, it partnered with WWF (the World Wildlife Fund) to work on challenges in freshwater conservation. Critics accuse these companies of "whitewashing" their corporate profits.

Creating shared value

In the past decade, another model for corporate social innovation has arisen, known as "creating shared value" (CSV). The term was coined by Michael Porter and Mark Kramer at Harvard Business School.[1] They declared that most corporate social responsibility programmes were short-sighted and misunderstood the deeper underlying value of social innovation. In their view, corporations maximise their competitiveness when they support the economic strength of their communities. Corporate profits and societal and economic progress are mutually dependent on each other.

The CSV model asserts that companies can find profitable innovations by intentionally trying to solve social or environmental problems. Just as the blue ocean strategy prompts innovators to look for new ideas in between established markets, the creating shared value model asks innovators to find marketable solutions in places where markets have traditionally failed.

There are three main areas of business where people seeking to create impactful innovators can create shared value. This is one recipe for social innovation.

1. **Reconceiving products and markets.** Innovators can reimagine their products and markets to meet social needs better. This might require a change of product features. Mobile phone operators Vodafone and its African arm Safaricom introduced M-PESA, a mobile phone-based service to transfer money for hundreds of millions of citizens who lack access to professional financial services, initially in Kenya and later across Africa and even in Asia and Eastern Europe. The service was designed to be simple, affordable, and did not require a bank account. In fact, it replaced bank accounts for the unbanked. M-PESA is now considered one the foremost success stories of financial inclusion. On the business end, M-PESA revenues had a ten-fold growth between 2010 and 2019 and account for about one-third of Safaricom revenues. Social value truly drove business value.

2. **Redefining productivity in the value chain.** Innovators can redefine their measure of productivity by considering their entire value chain to improve the quality, quantity, cost and reliability of their inputs and distribution of products or services in a sustainable manner. Women make up 60% of the world's workforce, but receive only 10% of the world's income. Through its Shakti initiative, Unilever provides women in rural India with accounting, sales and IT skills training needed to run an

entrepreneurial venture and both become financially independent and feel empowered. Tens of thousands of Shakti participants have become agents for Unilever, distributing its products to over 160,000 villages and more than 4 million households in rural India, and so earning a sustainable income. On the business end, Unilever now generates over $250m revenues from customers who were previously hard to reach, and sales have been growing consistently. Such inspiring results encouraged Unilever to train village women in Pakistan as beauticians using Unilever beauty products, redefining how and where value for all stakeholders is created in the value chain.

3. **Enabling local cluster development.** Innovators can embrace local economic development – formerly the domain of government entities – developing a strong competitive context, including reliable local suppliers, a functioning infrastructure, access to talent and an effective legal system. In Ivory Coast cocoa operations, Nestlé invests in plant research to create higher quality seedlings with higher yield, trains farmers to use improved crop and pest management techniques and ensures they meet the requirements for Fairtrade label certification, which guarantees higher revenues. Nestlé also builds schools and provides free education to farmers' children so that school becomes affordable and the risk of child labour is reduced.

   Nestlé's cocoa plan enables farmers to grow more and better cocoa, earn a higher income and improve social conditions. On the business end, 40% of Nestlé global expenditure for raw materials is for just three ingredients:

milk, coffee and cocoa. Supply conditions for these commodities are often challenging: poorly paid farmers leave the fields to seek more lucrative employment in cities, causing a shortage of labour and skills that results in lower supply, and poor infrastructures in supplier countries that also threaten the quality and quantity of cocoa beans. The cocoa plan ensures a sustainable supply of high-quality cocoa for Nestlé. The creation of these powerful clusters of suppliers would not only improve the quality of the supply but also attract other companies such that the local cluster could train its labour force, increase its wages and reduce local poverty.

The power of the CSV framework is its approachability by all innovators. Whereas corporate social responsibility assumes that you run a corporation, creating shared value means offering advice to people who are just starting the design of their new idea at some point along the roadmap to a social innovation.

Benefit corporations

The evolution of CSR and CSV has fostered a new type of organisation that is founded on the expectation that it will deliver profits *and* social impact. Created in 2006, the non-profit company B Lab certifies companies that embrace social and environmental improvement with a "B" ("B" for beneficial) certification. The assessment evaluates a company's operations, supply chain and inputs and business model, along with its impact on its workers, community, environment and customers. Interest in the B certification has grown steadily. There are currently more than 4,000 B Corporations in 77 countries, with many well-known brands among them, including Patagonia, Ben & Jerry's, Danone, Bombas, New Belgium Brewing, Eileen Fisher and Lemonade, alongside thousands of small and medium-sized businesses.

Many governments followed suit, creating a new legal form of company, the B Corporation. Whereas traditional for-profit corporations have a legal obligation to maximise profits on behalf of shareholders, shareholders in B Corporations cannot force the company to maximise profits, but they can insist that the company optimise profits and impact together.

As you are contemplating a social innovation, you will eventually be confronted with some decisions about the legal

The fortune at the bottom of the pyramid

The CSV movement joins another movement championed by the late C.K. Prahalad at the University of Michigan and Stuart Hart at Cornell University that alerts innovators to the "fortune at the bottom of the pyramid".[2] The authors referred to the pyramid of economic wealth, where the widest point at the bottom is inhabited by 2 billion people who earn less than $2 per day. This strategy has two implications. The first is that innovators who can craft affordable solutions to bring these non-consumers into the market have an enormous potential customer audience. An innovator can earn a fortune by selling to this large audience. This implication also mirrors Christensen's theory of disruption through the creation of new markets. The second implication from a focus on the bottom of the pyramid is that these consumers also help to manufacture and deliver these innovations, earning wages and learning commercial skills. An innovator can help people at the bottom of the pyramid earn their own fortunes. This implication mirrors Porter and Kramer's emphasis on local clusters in the creating shared value model.

structure of the entity. B Corp status not only provides some useful protections under the law, but also gives innovators ideas about how to maximise the social impact of the company that will deliver the innovation.

Multiple innovations for social impact

Social innovation can happen at many levels – new philosophy (CSR), new strategy (CSV), new governance (B Corp) – but the most impactful innovations involve multiple innovations at the same time. One of the great success stories in social innovation, microfinance, offers a powerful illustration of the many innovative efforts towards creating value for many stakeholders in complex business ecosystems. Microfinance consists in providing credit and other financial services on a micro-scale, prevalently to unbanked or unbankable individuals who would otherwise be unable to access credit.[3]

Poor and unemployed people do not have the income, the assets and often even the personal identification documents required to do business with commercial banks. They are limited in their ability to accumulate any savings or access credit. For example, when Agora Microfinance started its operations in Zambia in 2011, only 37.3% of the 14.5 million population had an account with a financial institution and seven rural regions had no bank at all.

Lacking access to formal financial services means that when the unbanked save, insure themselves and borrow, they do so through informal and inefficient channels. For example, they participate in rotating credit schemes and burial societies and borrow from other unbanked relatives who can spare only small amounts or from loan sharks who charge exorbitant interest rates. These inefficient financial services make it hard for the unbanked to make the investments necessary to ensure a higher income. So they are caught in a vicious cycle of poverty.

Traditional commercial lenders screen borrowers to ensure they have an income sufficient to repay the loan and demand some asset as collateral, which they can seize in case of default. Microcredit, however, is targeted at unbankable borrowers. This entails major transaction costs: screening reliable borrowers when very little information about them is available, providing loans as low as $10, sometimes in inaccessible locations scattered across vast rural regions, and finally enforcing repayments in the absence of collaterals or through weak judicial and court systems. Two major innovations helped overcome these challenges: group lending and dynamic incentives.

Microloans were not offered to individual borrowers, but to groups whose members are jointly responsible for the repayment. This way, it was the borrowers who identified and grouped with reliable co-borrowers and whose loans they voluntarily take responsibility for. With group lending, more people can be held responsible for repayment and it stimulates a system of peer monitoring and social sanctioning, and larger amounts can be offered to the group rather than smaller amounts to individuals, making lending more sustainable.

Microfinance institutions also create dynamic incentives to repay, by not disbursing loans all at once. Groups receive the full loan amount only after they demonstrate the ability to pay it back right from the beginning. Frequent instalments also ensure that borrowers pay back their loans before they have the chance or the temptation to spend money otherwise.

This example serves as both an inspiration and a powerful reminder that innovation happens in context and social innovation happens in complex contexts, where multiple challenges require multiple innovations. Muhammad Yunus and the Grameen Bank, which he founded, were awarded the Nobel Peace Prize in 2006 for championing microfinance. Even more than this, they helped raise millions out of poverty and inspired thousands of social innovators to embark on similar journeys.

Where to begin?

Hearing about the examples of extraordinary social innovators like Professor Yunus can be inspirational and frustrating in equal measure. You may wonder whether you have got what it takes to achieve similar feats. The good news is that, yes, everyone can be a social innovator.

Several success stories around the world illustrate the different paths to identifying social needs, recognising opportunities, acquiring resources and developing solutions. Perhaps one of these models appeals to you.

- **Social bricoleurs.** Sometimes social innovators identify local, small-scale issues thanks to their intimate knowledge and understanding of local conditions and activate local resources to tackle them. Lebanese fashion designer Sarah Beydoun launched Sarah's Bags to help female prisoners earn a living by manufacturing high-end bags and other accessories. The idea occurred to her while conducting field work for her graduate degree in sociology, which put her in touch with female inmates.

Engaging with a problem she understood personally, and looking for a simple, readily available solution, Sarah started bringing sewing materials to prison. After graduation, while working for a local NGO teaching work skills to vulnerable women, she decided to launch her own enterprise. Now carried by global icons such as Beyoncé, Amal Clooney and Queen Rania of Jordan, Sarah's Bags helped Lebanese women support their families, overturn wrongful convictions, and even provide employment for other women in their communities. But it all began with a committed graduate student, responding to local conditions.

- **Social constructionists**. Social innovators do not need to be closely connected to a problem. Sometimes outsiders have the necessary perspective to identify market failures and spot opportunities. A lawyer and real estate investor, Shaffi Mather, founded the largest for-profit ambulance service in the developing world, Dial 1298 for Ambulance. After witnessing the timely and professional intervention of an ambulance that saved his mother's life while in New York, he determined to bring a similar service to his home country of India. To ensure the service would be financially sustainable but accessible, patients taken to private clinics pay more and so subsidise the cheaper or free rides to public hospitals for the poorest citizens. Every year, hundreds of 1298 ambulances save thousands of lives across India. Yet it all started with a real estate lawyer.

- **Social engineers**. Some social innovators identify global, systemic failures and carefully design new innovations to tackle these enormous challenges. The intensive animal farming model at the core of our food system is one of the most severe environmental problems in the world. Patrick Brown of Stanford resolved to tackle it. He launched Impossible Foods, a company that makes plant-based meat analogues, while using 25% of the water, 5% of the land, and emitting only about 10% of the greenhouse gases of animal meat.

This is not to suggest that social innovators must commit to one of three predetermined paths. On the contrary, social innovation journeys are open to multiple approaches and they are open ended. Even Professor Yunus started small. He began as a social bricoleur, lending $27 of his own money to 42 women merchants from a village near Chittagong University, where he was a professor in 1976. Many others, inspired by his model, took the social constructionist path and replicated microfinance in their countries.

Social incubators

Despite the opportunities available, social innovation can be more challenging than other kinds of innovation because the customers may be far away from the founders and because the indirect benefits of the product may initially be hard to measure and articulate. Fortunately, there are now thousands of incubator programmes that can help social innovators find and refine new solutions.

One of the earliest and visionary incubators was Ashoka, founded in 1981 to assist "changemakers" to develop transformative businesses that solve problems. Originally focused on social innovation within the United States, Ashoka now operates in more than 90 countries and has worked with nearly 4,000 social entrepreneurs. Ashoka seeks to develop not just innovators but change-makers with direct training and access to its network of Ashoka Fellows who support each other and champion other innovative new ideas.

EBN (the European Business and Innovation Centre Network) sponsors the Transnational Network for Social Innovation Incubation, an association tasked to develop a network of successful social incubators throughout Europe. Dozens of incubators and accelerators also exist in the Middle East, India and throughout Africa and Asia. Deloitte's DASI (Deloitte Accelerator for Social Innovation) programme in the Middle East sponsors a regional competition across 13 countries to select two winners that will receive mentorship and skills development. Numerous private foundations also offer awards, such as the prestigious Skoll Award for Social Innovation that searches for successful social enterprises that have already had an impact on the world. Each year, six winners receive an investment of $1.5 million paid out over three years to enable them to scale up their activities and increase their impact.

Many corporations have themselves incubated social innovations. In 2007, for instance, pharmaceutical giant Novartis spun off Arogya Parivar ("healthy family") to market less expensive drugs to millions of India's poor at the bottom of the pyramid. The company identified eleven drugs that could be packaged differently and sold at a more affordable price. The spin-off was also able to create its own network of distributors and hire hundreds of local educators to teach the public about health and medical treatment. Arogya Parivar was not expected to show a profit for years, so Novartis funded it through seed funds from its social business group. The venture has proven very successful and has been adapted into Kenya, Indonesia and Vietnam.

Two more tools for social innovators

Our own research has generated two additional suggestions.[4]

Social innovators leverage their own and their customers' social networks to find people who would benefit from a particular service.

You might recall from the discussion on disruptive innovation the example of Solar Sister, which employs female entrepreneurs to sell solar- and battery-powered lanterns in parts of Africa. The typical customer in the regions where the company operates is a female head of the household. The female salespeople empathise and connect with the female customers. Even more powerfully, the salespeople are trained to start with their own networks to connect with people who already have an introduction and a bond of trust. Because these solar lanterns are life-changing innovations, these customers then connect the salespeople to even more people. This emphasis on personal networks applies to the sale of any kind of product, but is especially vital for social innovations, which can often be more complex or emotionally valuable than for-profit staples.

Social innovators do not necessarily need to convince their customers to change their behaviours or expectations.

Instead, clever innovators design products that fit into the same "hole" in a customer's life to create an incremental improvement in value. However, these products employ a dramatically different method to deliver value that the customer might not even see. For example, in Tanzania, people travel to their local village centre to purchase containers of kerosene each week, which they transport home to use as a cooking fuel. EGG-energy (where EGG stands for "engineering global growth") offered batteries for rent in these same village centres, which power electricity-based cook stoves and lanterns. Customers bring the depleted batteries back to the village centre for recharging, just as they would have returned an empty kerosene jug. The EGG-energy solution has a slightly better price and performance than kerosene from the customer's point of view. The fact that it is significantly more environmentally friendly than the extraction and distillation of pollution-causing petrochemicals is not a value proposition that the EGG-energy founders necessarily need to explain to customers. The company's profitability and its social impact move upwards together.

The future of social innovation

The movement to find and launch social innovations has continued to expand under the labels of the "green economy", "business with a purpose", "stakeholder capitalism", "philanthropic capitalism" and "net positive capitalism". There is a growing consensus that corporations have a duty to society to engage actively with some of the world's most pressing social and environmental problems. A study by polling firm Certus in 2019 indicted that 70% of consumers say they want to buy goods from companies that address social and environmental issues and 46% say they pay close attention to a company's efforts to be socially responsible.

Food companies like Nestlé, Unilever and Danone and car companies like Nissan and Toyota have re-cast their self-defined role in society to encompass not just their products but also their impact on people. Nestlé now views itself as a purveyor of health products. Danone's CEO Franck Riboud redefined the company to be a provider of nutrition, which encouraged the firm to sell off its beer, meat and cheese units and focus on water, dairy products and even medical nutrition.

The pressure for corporations to participate in social innovation is unlikely to wane. Many voices today are calling for companies to establish a more just and sustainable balance between economic efficiency, ecological preservation and social equity. This pressure reveals a demand among consumers for products and services that innovate for profit and impact together – that is, products and services that create value according to a definition of value that is way more ambitious and far reaching.

We opened this chapter with a report on the plastic waste that is accumulating in several oceans around the world, aggregated by ocean currents into a gyre of visible and invisible particles of pollution. This gyre is a clear manifestation of a market failure. There is no concentrated, specific, immediate incentive for individuals to reduce their plastic litter.

A start-up in Oakland, California is endeavouring to change this. Kamilo's solution applies location-tracking and blockchain technologies to recycled plastic in order to determine who is recycling and who is not. This accountability could also create new opportunities for companies that use recycled plastic to earn money by selling carbon offsets in recognition that recycled plastic generates less greenhouse gas than creating new virgin plastic.

The two founders of Kamilo are scientists and activists. Yes, they hope to change the world by empowering accountability for all kinds of natural resources. To start, they are working with their local town recycling centre to track a few hundred pounds of plastic through production, use, recycling and reuse. They demonstrate that dedicated, ambitious, disciplined people can envision and launch social innovation. Indeed, that is the only way these innovations emerge.

Epilogue: Improving innovation for ever greater impact

If you've chosen to read this book, you understand that missing out on innovation is risky. We wanted to write a book about hope, inspiration and guidance.

This is the age of innovation. Yet innovation is broken: 75% of new products fail; 90% of start-ups fail. Enormous amounts of resources are wasted in the process. These resources could generate immense value for the entire world if they were better managed.

Innovation is not an occasional effort or a serendipitous event. It is a long-term commitment to cultivating the right mindset, developing the right culture, mastering the right tools and methods, and pursuing the right trajectories. We never suggested it's easy. We did suggest, however, that it is for everyone.

The spectrum of innovation we've covered has been broad – and we hope has provided you with myriad insights into how you might approach developing an innovation project in your company, start-up or nonprofit. In the opening of the book, we presented you with what we called the innovation pyramid, and we have now covered it from bottom to top.

To survive and thrive everyone needs to innovate more and better. In this book we explained how to do so, step by step up to the summit of the innovation pyramid.

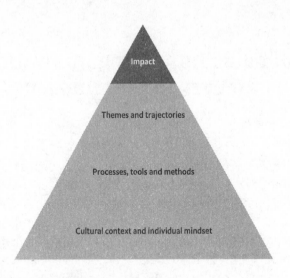

Domino effect of innovation

At the top of the pyramid is *impact*. Innovation that achieves impact can fuel the success of millions of companies, improve the conditions of life for vast segments of humanity, and change the world environmentally, socially and politically.

Innovation is good for everyone. It improves productivity and reduces costs. This means we can use our scarce resources to do more, help more users meet more of their needs, and so earn more resources that we can invest into further innovation. Innovation makes organisations more competitive – that is, they can seize a bigger share of the pie than their competitors who lag behind. But it is not a zero-sum game. We defined innovation as creating value. This means it enlarges the pie to the benefit of many stakeholders. This is the impact we envision.

The impact we see today is only a beginning. Everything

about innovation that this book has covered is neither fixed nor immutable. Innovation is a dynamic process and we all can count on new methodologies, processes, business models and markets for innovation to come about without end. What is fascinating about innovation is that it continuously feeds itself. The impact of a disruptive or radical innovation especially can set off a surprise domino effect that becomes the basis for another innovation or series of innovations.

In Chapter 8 we discussed bitcoin, the cryptocurrency that has increasingly become the new "gold standard" for currency exchange because it is difficult if not impossible to hack, cheat or commit fraud with. The backbone of bitcoin is blockchain, a digital ledger of transactions that is shared across a huge network of computer systems around the world. Given that the keepers of the blockchain are so widespread and they exchange the ledger in microseconds, it is almost impossible to cheat on a transaction or steal currency from the blockchain.

It is now becoming clear that blockchain technology has far-reaching uses as innovative new business opportunities emerge. The blockchain approach to managing many other types of data beyond currencies could remove the power that some companies amass when they own the data privately. Imagine how certain types of data might be held by the "public". This could mean that Facebook or Amazon would not have a competitive advantage if the gazillion bits of data they control were in the public domain so that others had access to it. Blockchain technology can also remove the need for intermediaries for various transactions. For instance, you may no longer need a third party to hold and validate your home's title. You may not even need a bank. Various government regulators might have less power because blocks and contracts can technically occur outside jurisdiction as the internet is global. Governments will need to rethink how to collect taxes on property sales, title and deed recordings, and other avenues by which they collect taxes.

And that's not the end of the potential innovations in property because of further domino effects. If the blockchain shows who has an asset and who needs an asset and smart contracts can automatically connect the buyer and seller without a commission, estate agents will need to find an innovative way to create value. It might also be possible that a property blockchain could put Airbnb out of business – ironically, one of the platform innovations that itself has altered the entire hotel industry and has been considered a leader in innovation.

Blockchain is just one technology that could open the door to a cascading series of innovations that no one has yet imagined. It is the stuff of science fiction, which is another reminder that as humans explore further and further out into space, we can expect innovations that only appear in sci-fi books right now.

Now what?

In its 2021 survey on innovation, the consulting firm Deloitte investigated the type of innovation efforts that have positive impacts on organisations. Based on these, it makes three recommendations that strongly resonate with everything we have written so far: get going, keep going, let go.

- **Get going**. Successful innovation is a hands-on exercise. You cannot innovate by thinking or running meetings.

This book can give you inspiration, structure and guidance. Yet reading it will not automatically make you innovate.

You must go *now*. Impactful innovators have a formal innovation programme or plan and the longer it has been running, the more successful it is. The advice here is similar to the advice for those who want to improve their health: start training. The best time to start training was ten years ago. The next best time? Right now.

You must go *big*. You surely can start with a small, tentative pilot. But a small pilot will not inspire people and organisations to drive innovative change. Impactful innovation requires resources, time, talent and a clear mission.

You must go *together*. Innovation is not a lonely enterprise. It requires diversity of perspectives and the support of many partners. Impactful innovators bring onboard C-suite leaders, customers, peers, even competitors if necessary.

- **Keep going**. Everyone is excited on the first day of class. It's only when the first assignments come in that stress kicks in. Innovation initiatives are accompanied by announcements and fanfare. But innovation happens only after overcoming setbacks. By its very nature, it entails failure. Innovation requires doing new things, doing new things requires learning, learning entails mistakes. Among entrepreneurial communities, fail fast is mantra. Not so much because entrepreneurs enjoy failure, but because they understand that mistakes are essential to learning and that failure is not the opposite of success, but its precondition. There are no quick wins in innovation.

- **Let go.** Despite aiming throughout this book to provide detailed guidance for your innovation efforts, innovation is most effective when it is let loose. Micromanagement and over-management are the greatest threats to impactful innovation. Innovation is a learning journey. It occurs at its best when it is allowed to progress with a clear goal and a clear process, but with flexible margins to deviate.

As we've repeated from the start, none of these efforts is easy. But neither do they require any special skill or resource. They are accessible to everyone.

Of bicycles and surfboards: homage to Baron Karl von Drais

Almost exactly 200 years after Karl von Drais invented the *laufmaschine* out of a straight wooden board between two wheels in Germany, Kyle Doerksen created a device from a straight board and a single wheel in Santa Cruz, California. Using a battery and sensors, the Onewheel is a "self-balancing" transportation vehicle. Someone standing on the board only needs to lean forward for the device to start moving forward. The rider leans back to slow down, and leans back more to move in reverse. The device itself learns the rider's habits to customise and improve its performance through data analysis.

The device itself emanated from Doerksen's experience with design thinking. He introduced the idea to potential customers on Kickstarter, the multi-sided platform that encourages a community of technophile early adopters to purchase products that have not even yet been manufactured at scale. The Onewheel is a manifestation of multiple processes and trajectories colliding into a single innovation that has already had significant impact for individual mobility.

We can't say it will change the world as much as the bicycle, the motorcycle or the car, but who knows? One day it might be the way that humans move about in areas of the planet where there are few roads or perhaps when humans arrive on the moon or Mars. It is an innovation that has large potential impact. And that is the goal you should seek.

Go innovate, with impact.

Notes

Chapter 1: Innovative people

1. G.T. Lumpkin and G.G. Dess, "Clarifying the entrepreneurial orientation construct and linking it to performance", *Academy of Management Review,* 21(1) (1996), pp.135–72.
2. T. Ladd, P. Hind and J.T. Lawrence, "Entrepreneurial orientation, Waynesian self-efficacy for searching and marshaling, and intention across gender and region of origin", *Journal of Small Business & Entrepreneurship*, 31(1) (2018), pp.1–21.
3. A. Bandura, *Self-efficacy: The Exercise of Control* (W.H. Freeman, 1997).
4. J. Hawkins, *A Thousand Brains: A New Theory of Intelligence* (New York: Basic Books, 2021).

Chapter 2: Innovative organisations

1. Kodak's former head of marketing intelligence revealed that he even conducted a market research study in 1981 after Sony commercialised its first fully electronic camera. The study predicted that digital cameras would take another ten years to catch on and compete with the quality of photographic film.
V. Barabba, *The Decision Loom: A Design or Interactive Decision-Making in Organizations* (Axminster, UK: Triarchy Press, 2011).

2. Forbes: www.forbes.com/sites/chunkamui/2012/01/18/
   how-kodak-failed/?sh=482ec6456f27
   CNN: www.cnn.com/2020/08/04/business/kodak-history-
   pharmaceutical-production/index.html
   Business Insider: markets.businessinsider.com/news/
   stocks/kodak-stock-price-765-million-government-loan-
   investigation-update-2020-12

3. M. Baghai, S. Coley and D. White, *The Alchemy of Growth:
   Practical Insights for Building the Enduring Enterprise* (New
   York: Perseus Publishing, 1999).

4. C.A. O'Reilly III and M.L. Tushman, "Organisational
   ambidexterity: past, present, and future", *Academy of
   Management Perspectives*, 27(4) (2013), pp.324–38.

5. "Your strategy needs a strategy", Boston Consulting Group,
   www.bcg.com/publications/collections/your-strategy-
   needs-strategy/intro

6. M. Reeves et al., "Ambidexterity: the art of thriving in
   complex environments", Boston Consulting Group
   (February 19th 2013), www.bcg.com/publications/2013/
   strategy-growth-ambidexterity-art-thriving-complex-
   environments
   K. Haanaes, M. Reeves and J. Wurlod, "The 2% company",
   Boston Consulting Group (February 20th 2018), www.bcg.
   com/publications/2018/2-percent-company

7. D.K. Rigby et al., "Agile innovation", Bain & Company (April
   19th 2016), www.bain.com/insights/agile-innovation/

8. F. Laloux, *Reinventing Organisations: A Guide to Creating
   Organizations Inspired by the Next Stage in Human
   Consciousness* (LannooCampus, 2016).

9. D.J. Teece, G. Pisano and A. Shuen, "Dynamic capabilities

and strategic management", *Strategic Management Journal*, 18(7) (1998), pp.509–33.
10. Deloitte report, *Design Principles for Building a Successful Corporate Accelerator;* and R. Eager, P. Webster and P. Kilefors, "The next generation of corporate incubators", Arthur D. Little, www.adlittle.com/en/insights/prism/next-generation-corporate-incubators

Chapter 3: Innovation as disruption

1. For a comprehensive summary of the theory, see C.M. Christensen, M.E. Raynor and R. McDonald, "What is disruptive innovation?", *Harvard Business Review*, 93(12) (2015), pp.44–53, hbr.org/2015/12/what-is-disruptive-innovation
2. C.M. Christensen, M.E. Raynor and R. McDonald, "What is disruptive innovation?", *Harvard Business Review*, 93(12) (2015), pp.44–53, hbr.org/2015/12/what-is-disruptive-innovation
3. T.S. Teixeira and G. Piechota, *Unlocking the Customer Value Chain: How Decoupling Drives Consumer Disruption* (New York: Currency, 2019).
4. A. Lanteri, M. Esposito and T. Tse, "From fintechs to banking as a service: global trends banks cannot ignore", LSE (January 19th 2021), blogs.lse.ac.uk/businessreview/2021/01/19/from-fintechs-to-banking-as-a-service-global-trends-banks-cannot-ignore/

Chapter 4: Innovation as a process

1. A great resource by IDEO is available at www.designkit.org
2. R. Fitzpatrick, *The Mom Test: How to Talk to Customers and*

Learn If Your Business Is a Good Idea When Everyone Is Lying to You (Robfitz Ltd, 2013).

3. C.M. Christensen et al., "Know your customers' 'jobs to be done'", *Harvard Business Review*, 94(9) (2016), pp.54–62.

4. "433 startup failure post-mortem", CB Insights (2022), www.cbinsights.com/research/startup-failure-post-mortem, accessed October 14th 2022.

5. "The rise & fall of design thinking at Oticon", thisisdesignthinking.net/2015/05/the-rise-fall-of-design-thinking-at-oticon/

6. W.C. Kim and R. Mauborgne, *Blue Ocean Strategy: How to Create Uncontested Market Space and Make the Competition Irrelevant* (Harvard Business Review Press, 2015), expanded edition.

Chapter 5: Refining innovation

1. S. Blank, "Why the lean start-up changes everything", *Harvard Business Review*, 91(5) (2013), pp.63–72.

2. E. Reis, *The Lean Start-Up: How Today's Entrepreneurs Use Continuous Innovation to Create Radically Successful Businesses* (New York: Crown Business, 2011) p.27.

Chapter 6: Innovative pricing

1. Most of these models and several more business model innovations are discussed in: O. Gassmann, K. Frankenberger and M. Csik, *The Business Model Navigator: 55 Models That Will Revolutionise Your Business* (Pearson, 2014).

2. P. Thiel and B. Masters, *Zero to One: Notes on Start-Ups, or How to Build the Future* (New York: Currency, 2014).

Chapter 7: Multi-sided platforms

1. The term "sharing economy" itself is embroiled in controversy as an oxymoron. Sharing traditionally does not involve compensation; there is no "economy" when people share. The popularity of the term has surreptitiously required that we redefine sharing as an act that allows multiple people to use the same asset, with or without compensation.
2. A. Osterwalder and Y. Pigneur, *Business Model Generation: A Handbook For Visionaries, Game Changers, and Challengers* (Hoboken, NJ: John Wiley & Sons, 2010).
3. M.M. Allweins, M. Proesch and T. Ladd, "The platform canvas – conceptualization of a design framework for multi-sided platform businesses", *Entrepreneurship Education and Pedagogy*, 4(3) (2021) pp.455–77.
4. For a full discussion of platform design, see K.J. Boudreau and A. Hagiu, "Platform rules: multi-sided platforms as regulators". In A. Gawer (ed.) *Platforms, Markets and Innovation* (Cheltenham, UK: Edward Elgar Publishing, 2009).

Chapter 8: Data-driven innovation

1. W. Knight, "Meet the Chinese finance giant that's secretly an AI company", *MIT Technology Review*, June 16th 2017, www.technologyreview.com/2017/06/16/151178/ant-financial-chinas-giant-of-mobile-payments-is-rethinking-finance-with-ai/
2. "Diaper–beer syndrome", Forbes, April 6th 1998, www.forbes.com/forbes/1998/0406/6107128a.html#7948c6b66260

3. C. Duhigg, "How companies learn your secrets", *New York Times Magazine*, February 16th 2012, www.nytimes.com/2012/02/19/magazine/shopping-habits.html?pagewanted=1&_r=1&hp

4. D. Carr, "Giving viewers what they want", *New York Times*, February 24th 2013, www.nytimes.com/2013/02/25/business/media/for-house-of-cards-using-big-data-to-guarantee-its-popularity.html

5. "The world's most valuable resource is no longer oil, but data", *The Economist*, May 6th 2017, www.economist.com/leaders/2017/05/06/the-worlds-most-valuable-resource-is-no-longer-oil-but-data

6. A. Lanteri, *Clever: The Six Strategic Drivers for the Fourth Industrial Revolution* (Lioncrest, 2019).

7. GPT-3, "A robot wrote this entire article. Are you scared yet, human?", *Guardian*, September 8th 2020, www.theguardian.com/commentisfree/2020/sep/08/robot-wrote-this-article-gpt-3

8. M. Subramaniam, "The 4 tiers of digital transformation", *Harvard Business Review*, September 21st 2021, hbr.org/2021/09/the-4-tiers-of-digital-transformation

9. A quick win or even a series of quick wins will not be enough to transform a company or to innovatively create value in the long run. One should, at the same date, invest in the capabilities to scale ambitions.

Chapter 9: Social innovation

1. M. Porter and M.R. Kramer, "Creating Shared Value", *Harvard Business Review*, Jan–Feb 2011, hbr.org/2011/01/the-big-idea-creating-shared-value

2. C.K. Prahalad, *The Fortune at the Bottom of the Pyramid: Eradicating Poverty through Profilts* (Wharton School Publishing, 2005).

3. The model of microfinance described here is the traditional version of microcredit. There now exist innumerable variants, for example without group lending, and extensions to this model. For example, microfinance institutions are increasingly offering savings accounts and affordable micro-insurance products. Sometimes, these products are bundled with credit. For example, some lenders set aside part of the regular loan repayments in a savings account, which becomes a collateral in case of default. After the borrower repays the loan, he can access the accumulated savings.

4. T. Ladd, "The embedded enterprise", *Stanford Social Innovation Review,* Spring 2015, ssir.org/articles/entry/the_embedded_enterprise

Index

Locations for illustrations or figures are entered in *italics*

platforms 133 *see also* multi-sided
  platforms
podcasts 99
Pole, Andrew 154
pollution 177–8, 180–81
Porter, Michael 184, 188
Prahalad, C.K. 188
prediction 160–61, 174
Pret A Manger 86, 87
pricing 114–16
  bicycles 57
  commission and 141–2
  freemium model 115
  lock-in and 118–21
  Marriott 162–3
  Netflix 60
  network monopolies 144
  price elasticity 114
  Starbucks raises 88
  supermarkets 71, 74
  see also revenue models
primary education 178–9
printers 119, 126–7
proactivity 14, 17
process
  agile processes 40
  beginning of 58, 74
  blue ocean strategy 90
  design thinking 75–6, 81, 84–5
  hypotheses 91, 95, 97, 105
  innovation as 4, 47, 92
product delivery 64
Proesch, Markus 136
profit
  core business 32
  hockey stick projections 124

Kodak 29
Laloux 42
lean start-ups 100, 104
mountain bikes 57
Netflix 60
network monopolies 144
protein folding 166
prototypes 80–81, 92, 93
pyramid notion 4–6
  diagrams 5, 9, 53, 200
  fortune at the bottom 188
  step-by-step 199

Q
quick wins 175, 204
Quirky 48

R
R&D departments 64–5
Raden 44
radical innovation 64–7
Radiohead 128
Rania, Queen (Jordan) 192
ratings 139
razor blades 118
reactive innovation 17
recharging stations 66–7
regulators 145–6, 150
reinforcement learning 157, *158*
Reis, Eric 92–3
Rent the Runway 123
Research & Development
  departments (R&D) 64–5
Research in Motion 30, 34
retail 155
retrosynthesis 166

About the authors

Ted Ladd is a Professor of Entrepreneurship and former Dean at the Hult International Business School, based on its San Francisco campus, where he teaches and researches ways to increase the impact of innovation. He also teaches innovation at Harvard University and Stanford University. He has participated in six different start-ups in Silicon Valley, mostly related to consumer software. The most recent was acquired by Google as the foundation for its Wear OS smartwatch ecosystem. He holds degrees from Case Western Reserve, Wharton at the University of Pennsylvania, SAIS at Johns Hopkins and Cornell University. He and his wife live in Jackson Hole, Wyoming.

Alessandro Lanteri is Professor of Strategy and Innovation at ESCP Business School and teaches executive education programmes for the University of Oxford's Saïd Business School and London Business School. An expert educator, he helps executives and students navigate turbulent environments and seize the opportunities of innovation. He works with multinationals, governments, international organisations, start-ups and family businesses across five continents. He holds a PhD from Erasmus University Rotterdam and an MSc from Bocconi University, and studied at Stern Business School (NYU), Saïd Business School, MIT, Stanford University and Harvard University. His research regularly appears in *Harvard Business Review* and *MIT Technology Review*. He is the author of *CLEVER: The Six Strategic Drivers for the Fourth Industrial Revolution*.